D0945050

LOOS
1915

LOOS 1915

PETER DOYLE

For Kitchener's volunteers

First published 2012 by
Spellmount, an imprint of
The History Press
The Mill, Brimscombe Port
Stroud, Gloucestershire, GL5 2QG
www.thehistorypress.co.uk

British Library Cataloguing in Publication Data.
A catalogue record for this book is available from the British Library.

ISBN 978 0 7524 7933 0

Typesetting and origination by The History Press
Manufacturing Managed by Jellyfish Print Solutions Ltd
Printed in Malta by Gutenberg Press.

CONTENTS

ACKNOWLEDGEMENTS

In attempting to write a readable introduction to the subject, I owe a debt to those authors who have endeavoured before me; I am particularly grateful for the rich legacy left by Sir James Edmonds' remarkably lucid official account. I am also grateful for contemporary accounts written by authors who served: Patrick MacGill in *The Great Push* (1915); Ian Hay in *The First Hundred Thousand* (1915); and James Norman Hall in *Kitchener's Mob* (1916). I thank Nigel Wilkinson, of the London Irish Rifles, for his hospitality and the chance to examine the football of Loos, and for permission to use images of the London Irish; Paul Reed for his support; and Paul Evans for his companionship on a damp day on the battlefield. Julie and James are my greatest support. Thanks also to Jo de Vries for her enthusiastic interest. Other than those I've taken or that are from my collection, the illustrations have been gathered from the pictorial publications of the day. Particularly important are *The War Illustrated* (Amalgamated Press), *The Illustrated War News* and *The Manchester Guardian History of the War*. I am also grateful for access to the free online resources of the Great War Picture Archive and the Library of Congress. The Loos battlefield is still strangely disturbing, even today. Industry and battle scarred, the clouds hang heavily over this part of French Flanders, often ignored by most who travel to the modern city of Lens or on to Arras. A pause here will repay the curious.

LIST OF ILLUSTRATIONS

INTRODUCTION

'You bloody cowards, are you leaving me to go alone?'… 'Not cowards, sir. Willing enough. But they're all f—ing dead.'

Lt Robert Graves, *Goodbye to All That*

The Battle of Loos (pronounced 'Loss'), fought in September–October 1915, is still a relatively unstudied corner of the Great War. For some time, the focus of British military historians and family genealogists has been on two sectors of the Western Front: the Ypres Salient of 1915–18 (likened to Britain's Verdun and the scene of at least four major battles) and the Somme battlefields of 1916. Today, thousands of people make the Channel crossing to visit these two regions, the people of Flanders and Picardy there to welcome them. Yet, between these two war-torn regions sits a less well-visited area of British and Commonwealth endeavour, a line of trenches that stretched from the southern shoulder of the Ypres Salient to Vimy Ridge. Flat, dreary and quite often rain sodden, visitors usually hurry through this area of French Flanders on their way to the delightful city of Arras, or farther onwards to the rolling chalk downlands of the Somme. Yet it was in this sector that the major British offensive efforts on the Western Front of 1915 were expended, and within which many tens of thousands of British lives were lost. Here too were the brickstacks of Cuincy, the canal at La Bassée, the village of Laventie immortalised in so many post-war accounts; here also were fought the battles of Neuve Chapelle, Aubers Ridge, Festubert and Loos. Commonwealth War Graves Commission cemeteries dot this landscape in testimony to the sacrifices made there. Though ill-fated, these 1915 campaigns would nonetheless shape British military thinking, and would cause great changes on the Home Front – yet they are still vaguely formed in the mind of the average battlefield visitor.

Why so? Much folklore about the Great War is focused upon the events of 1916–17 and the 'lost generation', the flower of British youth, swept aside on the battlefields of the Somme. Most modern historians contest this image, citing dry statistics to demonstrate that just over 11 per cent of those who joined died, but despite this there is evidence to suggest that loss became commonplace and bereavement a matter of fact. Fighting a rear-guard action against what could be termed the 'lost generationists', many historians are also committed to turning around that other juggernaut, the concept of 'Lions led by Donkeys', the incompetence of British 'Chateau Generals' all too willing to send their men 'up the line to death'. Founded in post-war disenchantment, this popular image of British incompetent generalship, of 'butchers and bunglers', first gained momentum in the 1960s, following the publication of Alan Clark's *The Donkeys* (1961), a controversial book that lambasted the efforts of 1915 and that was to inspire the Joan Littlewood stage production *Oh, What a Lovely War!* (1963). Roundly criticised and mostly discredited, the idea that all British generals were incompetent nevertheless finds currency today, with the television comedy *Blackadder Goes Forth* reviving the theme in 1989. There are signs that the juggernaut is starting to turn, however, and that the main focus of all of this ire, General Sir Douglas Haig, is being rehabilitated from ignorant 'donkey' to intelligent 'lion'.

In the 1980s, several historians developed a concept of the British Army in the Great War that became known as the 'learning curve'. The main focus was the conduct of the British Army during the closing stages of the war, the battles of the Hundred Days that commenced with the offensive at Amiens on 8 August 1918 and which were to drive the Germans back to their starting positions of September 1914. If the generals, Haig in particular, were so stupid, the men so poorly led, how could they achieve so much? The doctrine of the learning curve places the experience gained by the British offensives of 1915–17 on a parabolic rise that leads to the victory of 1918. Instead of the 'futility' expressed by the 'Donkeys', we now have the hope that the lives lost would amount to a meaningful purpose. This view was certainly sincerely held by many veterans, now all gone. Recent scholarship suggests the learning curve was, however, a somewhat sinuous curve, with many setbacks interspersed with advances in tactics and technology – referred to as revolutions in military affairs (or RMAs); the Battle of Loos marks one of the most important arcs in the early parts of the curve.

Loos has been the subject of several books over the last ten years, despite having been largely overlooked and even ignored in the wake of the publication of Alan Clark's polemic. The first attempt at a study was Philip Warner's collection of veterans' memories, widely criticised for not offering a view on the battle, but a valuable collection of memories nonetheless. More recently, three new studies of the battle have examined its progress in minute detail, and in particular the performance of the various divisions pitted against the German defences on 25–26 September and on its succeeding days. These books have marked in sometimes bewildering detail the movement of corps, divisions, brigades and battalions across the battlefield. For readers requiring an insight into such detail, I commend Brigadier General Sir James Edmonds' original *Official History* of 1928, which is written with lucidity and insight; and Nick Lloyd's careful step-by-step analysis of the major components of the battle, *Loos 1915*, published eighty years later in 2008. The purpose of the present book, however, is to provide a brief introduction based on the key issues, an introductory narrative to the battle. As such, I have attempted to keep the discussion of the separate units, corps, divisions, brigades and battalions as simple as possible.

What emerges from any study of Loos is that it was fought against the prevailing opinion of the British generals, against the view that the British Army should stand on the defensive on the Western Front until its citizen army was trained and ready for deployment to meet the Germans. However, at a time of growing crisis in the world war, with the Russian armies in Poland on the verge of collapse, it was also fought in support of the French and their desire to break the deadlock of positional warfare, following Joffre and Foch in their doctrine of the offensive. Similar circumstances would also prevail in the offensives fought by the British on the Somme in 1916 and at Arras in 1917. Loos was also fought against the concept of 'good ground'. In history, the lessons of fighting against instead of with terrain (comprising geology, topography, routes to the front and weather conditions) are clear; at Loos, these factors had a major role to play in the outcome of the battle. All these aspects are discussed in this book.

TIMELINE

10 March	Battle of Neuve Chapelle opens
13 March	Battle of Neuve Chapelle halted
22 April	Second Battle of Ypres opens
9 May	Battle of Aubers Ridge
19 May	Battle of Festubert
25 May	Second Battle of Ypres ends
20 September	XI Corps form up in reserve
21 September	Preliminary bombardment opens
25 September	First day of the Battle of Loos
25 September	French Tenth Army attacks south of Lens, opening of the Third Battle of Artois
25 September	Third Battle of the Champagne opens
25 September	21st and 24th divisions (XI Corps) moved up
26 September	Second day of the Battle of Loos; attack of the XI Corps fails
27 September	German counter-attack at The Dump and Hohenzollern Redoubt

Timeline

1915

28 September	Attack on Hill 70 and Chalk Pit Copse
28 September	High watermark of Third Artois Offensive
29 September	General Haig writes to Lord Kitchener to complain about French's handling of the reserves
3 October	Hohenzollern Redoubt retaken
13 October	Last actions of the Battle of Loos
4 November	End of the Battle of the Champagne
6 November	Official end of the Battle of Loos
10 December	General Haig replaces Field Marshal French as British commander-in-chief

HISTORICAL BACKGROUND

The ill-fated Loos offensive was undertaken directly against the opinion of Haig, the man who, as Commander of the First Army, had to carry it out.

Sir Basil Liddell-Hart, 1930

In 1915, the Entente Powers were on the back foot; the Germans were still in the ascendancy, fighting a holding war of position in the west, while forcing the Russians back in the east. In the opening days of the war, the Schlieffen Plan had been intended to knock France out, but the swinging door of the German Army had met the door jamb of the Marne, just in front of Paris. From this point on, the war was condemned to be a long engagement, and, as Kitchener would predict, it would last at least three years. On the Marne it was the French commander-in-chief, Joseph Joffre, who was to recall all reservists, famously ferried from Paris to the front in taxicabs by the order of General Gallieni. The French were to be joined by the British Expeditionary Force (BEF) in holding the enemy at a most critical point in the campaign. From this point on, and until the end of 1914, the battles that would become known as the 'Race to the Sea' would witness the two sides trying to turn the flank of the other in the traditional

1. The Belgian city of Ypres under bombardment, 1914.

cockpit of Europe – Flanders, the flat manoeuvring ground of European armies for centuries. This distinctive region of northern Europe stretches from the sand-dune-stretched littoral of France and Belgium to the chalk upland of Artois, and has seen warfare since the Middle Ages. Journeying to the south, the landscape of this flat and open region passes from the Belgian clay plain to the dowdy industrial chalk flats of French Flanders.

For the BEF, placed between what remained of the Belgian armies (reinforced by the French) at the coast of Flanders and the French armies in Artois, Flanders would become the place of battle for four years of a hard war. Ypres – now the Flemish-speaking town of Ieper – would be the centre of British endeavour, with battles there from late 1914 right the way

17

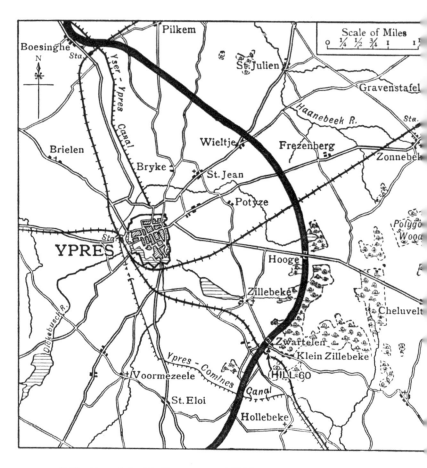

2. The Ypres Salient in the summer of 1915.

through to the end of the war in 1918. The First Battle of Ypres, in November–December 1914, was to form part of the 'Race to the Sea', with British regular troops (and some Territorials) holding on tenaciously in the face of a determined German Army. Here there would be waterlogged ground, hasty scrapes in the earth and the birth of the legend of the old BEF and its fire rate of

18

fifteen rounds a minute from Lee-Enfield rifles. With the German line held by the close of the year, the early part of 1915 saw the development of the tradition of trench warfare that has come to represent the Great War to so many people. Grimly holding on, the British toiled in and around the clay plain of Ypres, while the Germans set about holding the high ground that faced the town on three sides, part of the Ypres Salient.

This bulge, following the low rising hills to the east of the town, defined an arc with a long axis running approximately north–south, facing east–west. The salient had been born in November 1914, when the German attacks from Armentières to Nieuport ran out of steam. Running around the hills, the German line, and British line following it, passed southwards over its saddle back and down to the damp valley of the Lys and on to Armentières. Farther south, the line passed through French Flanders to the canal of La Bassée, in that flat tract of land between the Lys and the Scarpe rivers. South from this the line was in French hands and ran southwards to Noyon, before tracking westwards to Verdun and the St Mihiel Salient, from there arcing around to the Swiss frontier. Stabilised in late 1914, this line would form the linear fortress of the Western Front, scene of the titanic battles of 1916–18, and successive attempts to break the line and sweep to victory. However, in 1915, matters were complicated.

For the French, the occupation of their home soil by the Germans was a national disgrace. General Joffre, commander-in-chief of the French armies and hero of the Marne, was a strong character whose relationship with his British Allies was not always what it should have been. Commanding armies many divisions strong, it was obvious that Joffre and the French were the principal opponents of the Germans on the Western Front, with the BEF in a subsidiary role at this point in its history. Field Marshal Sir John French, the British commander, was ordered to maintain an independent command, yet was unable to act alone. Though having the power to organise and command his armies and their

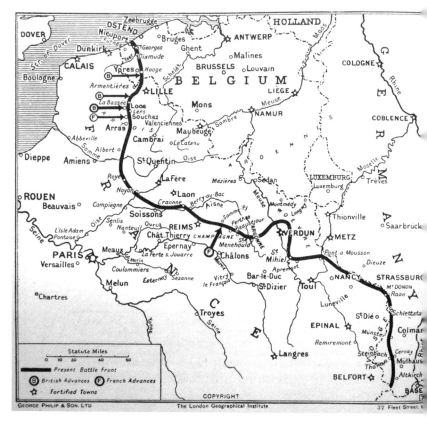

3. Map of the Allied front showing the Noyon Salient and the French (F) and British (B) plans to attack in Artois and the Champagne in 1915.

dispositions, the British commander would, in essence, have to bow to the pressures of his French ally to press the enemy line and force the Germans back.

With this in mind, General Joffre enacted plans in late 1914 and 1915 that would throw the might of the French Tenth Army at the Germans in Artois, close to the city of Arras, and particularly the natural stronghold of Vimy Ridge; while also committing the

French Fourth and Second Armies in the Champagne. In attacks that commenced in the winter of 1914–15 he hoped that the right-angled dogleg of the German front could be driven in, thereby allowing for mobile warfare to be resumed. This plan would form the basis of French planning throughout 1915 – and would see a vast toll of French casualties mount up in these war-blighted areas. Subsidiary to the might of the French armies, all the BEF could do was bob up and down on the line like flotsam brought in by the tide, yet still carrying out its main responsibilities – to support the French commander-in-chief while maintaining its guard on the Channel ports vital to both the protection of the BEF itself and to the defence of the coast of southern England, facing France across the Channel. This would mean a number of small offensives in 1915 north of La Bassée canal intended to support the French, at Neuve Chapelle in March 1915 and at Aubers Ridge and Festubert in May 1915. These attacks would all have two points in common: a lack of resources and reserves, and a certainty that any breakthrough would quickly be swallowed up by the envelope of the German Army.

For the British, their first taste of their own offensive came with the Battle of Neuve Chapelle, on 10 March 1915. Part of the general French strategy to try to break the German hold in French Flanders, it was largely unsupported. Despite its limitations, however, it nearly worked, with the British breaking through the line – a magnificent force of arms that was only to stall for want of artillery and ammunition. These would be repetitive themes in all British offensives fought throughout 1915. The limitations of this offensive did not deter the Allies, however, and at a meeting in Chantilly in late March the British commander-in-chief agreed to resume the offensive in Artois in May. Attacking once more to the north of La Bassée canal, there was hope that Aubers Ridge would be taken, thereby paving the way for cavalry exploitation. With even fewer resources than those available for the previous battle, this would be a faint hope indeed.

For their part, the Germans would also attempt to break the line in an offensive in Flanders; this would be fought at Ypres in April–May 1915, and would see the use of a new and terrible weapon of war, poison 'cloud gas' released from cylinders, employing the wind as a major contributor to the outcome of this warfare. When deployed at 5pm on 22 April 1915, the effect of the gas spreading across the Ypres battlefields was sufficient to drive French troops occupying the northern limb of the salient back in terror, losing around 6,000 killed to the asphyxiating effects of the chlorine gas. Nevertheless, its success came as a surprise to the Germans, who did not exploit the 4-mile gap that had opened in the line. Canadian troops of the British Second Army, clutching to their faces extemporised masks of cotton soaked in urine, held the line; Ypres was not to fall, and remained in Allied hands throughout the war.

While Second Ypres was being fought, the French continued to press their proposal to have Artois as the main offensive area, punching away at the German 6. *Armee* in an attempt to stove in the bulwark. With the French attacking Vimy Ridge to the south, to the north of La Bassée canal the British would once more take on the ground it had assaulted during Neuve Chapelle two months earlier. Here the British First Army under General Haig engaged in a battle, Aubers Ridge, which would become infamous for its lack of progress at high cost. However, with the French offensive in Artois rolling on, a new attack, this time on a

CHLORINE GAS

Chlorine gas kills by irritating the lungs so much that they are flooded, the victim actually drowning in their own body fluids. Men killed by gas show startling blueness of the lips and face, a function of the blood becoming starved of oxygen. These aspects became central motifs in Wilfred Owen's celebrated war poem *Dulce et Decorum est*.

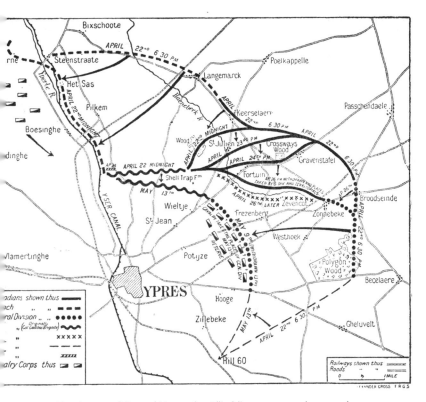

4. *Sketch map of Second Ypres; the Allied line was severely pressed on 22 April 1915.*

limited front, would be fought at Festubert, again with a similarly limited effect. Together, the combined first and second battles of Artois would cost the French at least 100,000 casualties, with an overall gain of a few miles of territory. It did not break the line; it would barely push the Germans back. The proposed breakthrough was indeed some way off. With this backdrop, it might possibly have been expected that the French would give up their aspirations to break through in Artois; but not in General Joffre's mind. Instead, the charismatic general made plans to carry out a third offensive to deliver the overall aim, comprising two titanic battles, again to be fought in Artois and the Champagne, once more with the aim of cutting off the knee of the Noyon Salient. While the Champagne would be solely a French affair, the Artois battle front would be an Anglo-French endeavour.

Facing General Sixt von Armin's *IV Armeekorps* (German *6. Armee*), the French Tenth Army would attack the Germans with seventeen divisions to the south of the substantial mining town of Lens, their front running from Arras northwards to this industrial centre. Well equipped with both artillery and ammunition, the French could expect that the opposing German trenches would be 'flattened'. However, like the British, the French were equipped primarily with field guns (with the famous 75mm gun being rightly celebrated and highly prised in infantry attacks), and the chances of dislodging their enemies from deep excavations were limited.

The BEF was allotted the sector north of the city of Lens, in the area south of La Bassée canal – south of the region they had assaulted earlier in the year. Here, three corps of the British First Army would be committed, comprising a mixture of regular and Territorial divisions, but leavened by three divisions of Kitchener's New Army. These New Army divisions were just starting to become available, but were of variable experience with most having just landed in France. The British would be seriously undergunned, however – a factor that was to hang over the British generals like a cloud. With the lost opportunities of Neuve Chapelle just months before fresh in the minds of Sir John French and his commanders, there were memories of the acute shortage of ammunition in this battle. This had led to the 'Shell Scandal', an affair splashed across the front pages of the popular British Northcliffe press that was ultimately to see the fall of the Liberal government and the creation of a new Ministry of Munitions.

The new ministry would have much to do in reshaping British munitions supply in the latter years of the war, but it would

THE SHELL CRISIS

In May 1915, the 'Shell Scandal' became front-page news. Colonel Repington reported in *The Times* that the attack at Aubers Ridge had failed due to a lack of shells: 'We had not sufficient high explosives to lower the enemy's parapets to the ground …The want of an unlimited supply of high explosives was a fatal bar to our success.' (*The Times*, May 1915) The 'Shell Scandal' of 1915 was to bring down the government and, with it, bring about the replacement of Winston Churchill as First Lord of the Admiralty. The main proposer of the campaign would hold his seat at the War Council, but not for long.

have little effect in the late summer of 1915; thus planning for a new offensive would mean careful husbanding of resources. This would be particularly important as the lessons of the earlier battles had shown that those fought on a narrow front, though concentrating effort at one point in the line, would also suffer the combined weight of enemy artillery fire on two sides, ranging across the battle front. With that in mind, the Battle of Loos would be fought on a much wider front than before, some 20 miles; expanding the front would decrease the effect of fire from both flanks sweeping the new line, but it would mean that there was a need for a much greater concentration of artillery fire in order to pursue the offensive. Yet in the summer of 1915, there was no way that this need could be met – unless, that is, there was another weapon that could be deployed. There was: gas. The British Government had sanctioned the use of gas as retaliation for the German attack in April 1915. With plans, research and manufacturing stepped up, Loos would see the first British attempt at a gas attack during the war.

General Joseph Joffre

General Joffre was the commander-in-chief of the French Army in the west. Joffre was a product of the *École Polytechnique* in Paris, and was to see through the siege of Paris during the Franco-Prussian War of 1870–71. Serving with the *Génie*, he was an engineer for much of his military career. Posted to numerous French colonies, he saw action in the controversial Keelung Campaign, fought in Formosa as part of the Sino-French War of 1884–85. However, it was as commander-in-chief of the French Army, an appointment from 1912 onwards, that was to cement his reputation. The appointment was not without controversy, however; Joffre had no direct experience of command at this level and had never served in a staff position. Nevertheless, with the painful experience of the defeat of 1871 still fresh, Joffre was committed to ensuring that the army was not defensively minded. With Germany still a perceived threat, in 1913 Joffre bought into Plan XVII, an idea developed by equally pugnacious General Ferdinand Foch as a means of dealing with their strong western neighbours. The plan required the invasion of Alsace-Lorraine, a territory taken from the French in the aftermath of the war of 1870–71. The plan made no account of the possibility of the German ideas of invading France through Belgium, however, and was therefore flawed.

With the outbreak of war seeing the development of the

Schlieffen Plan in northern France, the flaws in Plan XVII were very much in evidence. With the French reeling back from the German attempts to outflank the capital, it was Joffre who was able to muster his forces to take on the might of the advancing German Army, saving the capital and the nation at the Battle of the Marne in 1914.

5. General Joseph Joffre.

Combining three armies under the Governor of Paris, Joseph Gallieni (Joffre's mentor), Joffre was also ruthless in dismissing senior officers who had not displayed sufficient resolve in the face of an efficient and capable enemy. They were to be replaced by generals who would have a major role in the future direction of the French military campaigns in the west – such as Foch, Nivelle and Petain. As an engineer, Joffre was also to ensure that the great logistical issues of fighting the Marne were overcome.

In late 1914 and 1915, Joseph Joffre was committed to the offensive and particularly to the concept of the destruction of the German *6. Armee*, where the German line bent sharply eastwards at Noyon, forming an immense open salient. With the idea that simultaneous attacks in Artois and the Champagne would be hammer blows that would be difficult to repulse, he believed that there would be a breakthrough in this area, one that would allow the war of movement to resume, the Germans being pushed back and their *6. Armee* being left in the air. Joffre would not lose faith in this plan throughout 1915, and this would lead to three dramatic campaigns, in both regions, that would add up to a huge number of casualties. The failure of these campaigns would weaken Joffre's hold on the French command, his position further weakened by the titanic attempts of the German Army to break the line and 'bleed the French Army white' at Verdun in 1916. Following both Verdun and the Somme offensive of 1916, Joffre was promoted to *Maréchal* of France – but then removed to be replaced by the ill-fated Joseph Nivelle, one of Joffre's own masters of the offensive, on 13 December 1916. From then on, Joffre's position would be largely ceremonial, first as head of the French Military Mission to its hapless ally Romania, and then, in 1917, serving the same role to the USA. After the war, Joffre retired from active service in 1919 and joined the *Académie Française*. Joseph Joffre died in January 1931.

THE ARMIES

'Kitchener's mob' they were called in the early days of August, 1914, when London hoardings were clamorous with the first calls for volunteers. The seasoned regulars of the first British expeditionary force said it patronisingly, the great British public hopefully, the world at large doubtfully.

James Norman Hall, *Kitchener's Mob*, 1915

The British Army

When Britain went to war in 1914, it had a small but highly trained army. The army had been overhauled in 1881 to create sixty-one regiments, each allied directly with a county or region, with a home depot and two locally recruited regular battalions. Further reforms by Lord Haldane in 1908 granted regiments a Special Reserve Battalion (whose purpose was to gather recruits) and three locally raised Territorial battalions. Men serving as Territorials did so on the understanding that they would serve as part-timers engaged on home defence, with no overseas commitment. However, with the coming of war, most 'terriers' joined the colours for full-time service overseas and Territorial recruitment was placed on the same level as all the others.

6. Field Marshal Lord Kitchener, Secretary of State for War.

For the regular soldier, mobilised for war, there was the usual budget of training, six months with the third battalion at the base depot before being deployed into the first or second battalion. The regular army was to maintain its cachet throughout the war, and belonging to the first or second battalion of an infantry regiment was seen as a badge of honour. The regular battalions available at home in 1914 were to form six infantry divisions; each division was to have three infantry brigades, with each brigade in turn composed of four infantry battalions. Brigades rarely had more than one battalion from a given regiment. The typical infantry division of 1914 would also have a significant artillery presence and an attached cavalry squadron, as well as components from all the other arms and services required to keep it operating in the field, a massive undertaking with around 15,000 men in a typical, full-strength British division. The six original divisions were to form the BEF in 1914, the first four of them taking part in the retreat from Mons in 1914, the other two being present in France by September 1914. By the end of the war, the British Army had expanded from its original six to seventy-five infantry divisions.

When Field Marshal Earl Kitchener of Khartoum took over as Secretary of State for War in August 1914, he was quick to understand that this war would be costly in manpower. Not confident that the Territorial battalions could be sufficiently flexible to allow rapid expansion, Kitchener made a direct appeal to the public, his sights set on expanding the army by 500,000 men, with separate appeals, in 100,000 tranches, to be numbered successively K1, K2, K3, and so on. The 'First Hundred Thousand', or K1, were recruited within days of the appeal; two divisions of K1 men would serve at Loos. Kitchener was to issue four further appeals through the late summer and early autumn of 1914. The phenomenon most closely associated with the hothouse of recruitment in 1914–15 was the raising of 'pals' battalions by local dignitaries, 1,000 men strong. It was Lord Derby who suggested the raising of battalions of men of the 'commercial classes' in a letter published in the Liverpool press on 27 August 1914. In all, 144 pals battalions would be raised, enough for twelve infantry divisions of the K4 and K5 recruitment tranches. These men would serve on the Somme in 1916; it would be the men of K1 and K3 who would serve at Loos.

The first recruits to join Kitchener's New Army were forced to make compromises: little in the way of equipment, no uniforms, no barracks. In the early stages of the war, supply of arms, uniform and equipment to the enthusiastic recruits of Kitchener's army was a difficult task; the Kitchener battalions were to be fed, housed and equipped at the initial expense of the authority that raised them. This meant sourcing uniforms from official and even commercial suppliers at a time when the country was alive with such pleas along its length and breadth. As a consequence, recruits were more often than not clothed in civilian garb and, as training camps had not yet been formed or established, they found themselves still living at home. Kitchener's men 'went to war' training in flat caps and tweed suits with broom handles before simple uniforms were supplied in what has become known as 'Kitchener Blue' – blue serge in place of khaki.

The British Army had experienced a trying time since it had arrived in France in 1914. Ultimately, British and Commonwealth troops were to occupy 120 miles of the front, in the historically strategic zone that straddled the Belgian–French border, extending south deep into Picardy. Engaged from August 1914 at the Battle of Mons, the BEF was to grow in size and stature to become the backbone of the Allied effort in the closing months of 1918, in campaigns that defeated Imperial Germany – with 5,399,563 Empire troops employed on the Western Front alone, the majority from the UK. Nonetheless, in 1915, the British Army had yet to come to its full strength and was very much to be the junior partner to the French. This would affect the outcome of the campaigns during this difficult year.

Britain had entered the First World War with just four regular infantry battalions capable of forming an expeditionary force to serve in France. Its overseas commitments meant that other battalions were serving overseas, protecting the outposts of the Empire; there were also battalions of the Territorial Force, intended initially as primarily a force for home defence (though

7. The 18-pounder field gun, the standard British artillery piece of the war.

most men volunteered for overseas service), and later in the war, newly raised volunteer and conscript forces. There would also be regular cavalry regiments – which were to be chronically underused in their intended role during the war, together with the Territorial Force's own cavalry, the Yeomanry. By 1915, most of the regular and a large majority of the Territorial Force battalions were being deployed overseas, second-line Territorials taking the place of regular troops in some of the quieter outposts, thereby allowing the regular battalions to return home from war service.

In addition to the infantry, there were associated artillery and engineer units. The Royal Regiment of Artillery was composed of three components: the Royal Horse Artillery (RHA) and Royal Field Artillery (RFA) manned field guns (13- and 18-pounder flat-trajectory, rapid-firing guns), while men of the Royal Garrison Artillery (RGA) were equipped with howitzers and other heavy guns. In 1915, the co-ordination between the branches was rudimentary, and the garrison gunners were frequently out of touch with their field-gunner cousins. The main arm of the RFA was the 18-pounder quick-firing field gun, which had a maximum range of over 6,500yds and was capable of firing shrapnel, high-explosive and star shells; 10,000 would be produced during the war. Howitzers were designed to lob large-calibre shells with a high trajectory so that they might drop slap-bang into the enemy's trench systems. Such heavy siege guns would usually be crewed by gunners of the RGA, situated farther back from the frontline, though there were also RFA howitzer batteries. With increasing precision, from 1916 onwards artillerymen developed new ways of delivering their goods, with creeping and box barrages intended to provide a protective screen around those attacking, isolating those within from the attentions of the defenders outside the curtain of shellfire. However, in 1915 limitations on the amount or artillery and of ammunition made such advances difficult.

Gas warfare is most commonly associated in the modern mind with the 'horrors' of the trenches. Poison gas was deployed in an active sense in April 1915, when the Germans first used it during the opening phases of the Second Battle of Ypres. Early gases were chlorine and bromine released from cylinders, creating moving 'gas clouds' that would cause irreparable damage to the lungs; chlorine would corrupt the lung tissues and create a situation where a man would drown from the effects. (Later on more complex mixes, including the caustic mustard gas, promoting temporary blindness and severe burns, would be deployed in artillery shells as tactical weapons.) Primitive respirators were quickly extemporised from field dressings soaked in alkaline bicarbonate of soda, a solution capable of neutralising the chlorine gas. Later, in 1915, flannel hoods soaked in sodium hyposulphite ('Hypo Helmets') followed, replaced by more sophisticated versions with eyepieces and exhalent valves ('Phenate' (P) and 'Phenate-Hexamine' (PH) helmets). These nightmarish creations were officially known as tube helmets from the tube that had to be gripped in the mouth to allow the wearer to breathe out – but were more often known to soldiers as the 'goggle-eyed buggers with the tit' (a fact famously recorded by Loos veteran Robert Graves in his book *Goodbye to All That*). They were to be superseded, in the face of increasing sophistication of gas warfare, by the Small Box Respirator (SBR) in 1916, which had a facemask and tube connected to a 'box' filled with lime-permanganate granules. This mask was to prove highly effective and gas was to become just another weapon to be endured by the man in the trenches; but in 1915 it was still effective and widely feared.

The Royal Corps of Engineers were also ever present – their field companies had the job of field engineering, while tunnelling companies had to carry out the ancient task of sapping and mining, laying offensive charges beneath enemy fortifications that would be exploded at will. Road and jetty construction, light railway support, water supply and signalling would be other tasks

PERCY TOPLIS

Percy Toplis was a fraudster who after the war impersonated officers in order to commit fraud and impress women. His life was serialised in the 1980s in the controversial BBC TV series *The Monocled Mutineer*. Toplis was to serve at Loos as a stretcher bearer with the RAMC, and the TV programme depicts him in the trenches during the battle. In real life he was to be transferred to Gallipoli in its closing stages, there to contract dysentery, before serving in Salonika and Egypt, where he contracted malaria. Deserting from the army, he embarked on a life of crime that would see him gunned down by the police.

of this diverse corps. Ensuring that men survived their wounds was the responsibility of the Royal Army Medical Corps (RAMC), whose role was to care for the wounded and to evacuate them efficiently from the frontline to (as it was hoped by most soldiers) Blighty. The casualty chain was a long one, and soldiers would hope to receive their 'ticket' – a label that marked him for transportation on hospital ships bound for home.

The British Army Uniform and Equipment

The khaki (Hindi-Urdu for dust) Service Dress uniform worn by the troops was first developed in 1902 as a replacement for the traditional centuries-old red coat of the British infantryman. The Service Dress jacket was characteristically loose-fitting, with a turned-down collar, patches at the shoulder to bear the extra wear from the position of the rifle butt in action and four pockets with button-down flaps. Shoulder straps bore regimental insignia in the form of brass shoulder titles. Throughout the war, insignia were added to the sleeves of the ordinary soldiers – the non-officer 'other ranks' – including rank badges and specialist 'trade' badges (such as those for machine-gunners, scouts and so on); divisional insignia would be added later in the war.

Service Dress trousers had a narrow leg to be worn with puttees and wool socks, over which were worn the regulation field boot, which was roughly square-toed, produced in thick hide with the rough side out and heavily dubbined (waterproofed with tallow/oil mixture). Soles were cleated with metal studs which were hard on the feet while marching on the stone-block pavé roads of France. British soldiers went to war in an awkward khaki peaked cap with stiffened rim; in late 1914 the softer Winter Service Dress cap was issued, known universally as the 'Gor Blimey', with flaps that could be fastened under the chin for extra warmth. Unloved by sergeant majors, it would later be replaced by the issue of a simpler soft cap, although it would be the 'Gor Blimey' that would be worn at Loos.

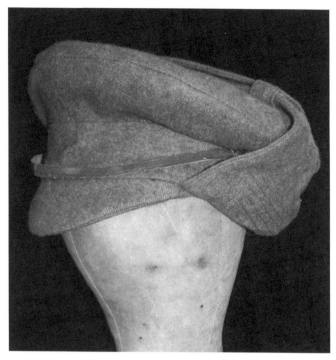

8. The British 'Gor Blimey' cap; properly the Winter Service Dress cap.

Officers' Service Dress consisted of a tunic with open step-down collar that was worn with shirt and tie (of all shades of khaki, according to taste), finished with a 'Sam Browne' belt (wide, brown leather belt, with diagonal strap over right shoulder). Distinct from their men, officers were easily identified by snipers, particularly when rank stars and crowns were worn in plain sight on the cuff. Some took it upon themselves to move these badges to the shoulder straps, or wear 'Tommy tunics' in battle, but this affectation was rare in 1915. Breeches of Bedford cord, a peaked cap and a variety of footwear were worn, from polished riding top boots and high-laced 'trench boots' to simple brown ankle boots and puttees. Officers similarly wore their equipment festooned

9 *A British second lieutenant of the Manchester Regiment,* c. *1915.*

about their person, supported by leather Sam Browne belt, and armed most commonly with a .455 calibre Mark VI Webley revolver, carried in a leather holster and with a lanyard.

10. A Scottish sergeant of the Seaforth Highlanders, in diced Glengarry cap.

Many of the Scottish battalions at Loos were kilted; the kilt was warm to wear with its many folds of woollen tartan, though the downside of the folds was their propensity to harbour lice, as well as their ability to soak up vast amounts of water. From late 1914 it was usual to wear it covered by a simple apron of khaki cloth. The highland soldier wore a range of caps and bonnets; early in the war the commonest was the Glengarry, which varied from plain dark blue to varieties with diced borders. For the 9th Division in the line at Loos, reinforcements would be arranged so that their Glengarry colours matched to avoid confusion. Other Scots at Loos would wear the khaki 'Tam O'Shanter', introduced in 1915.

Surviving in the open in all weathers meant warm clothing was a must. Though Loos was fought in the autumn, this part of Flanders is often cold and damp; greatcoats were worn into battle in some cases. Yet the issue greatcoat was cumbersome; more often than not it would be left in the transport lines. Instead, an outlandish, often multi-coloured, goatskin, sleeveless jerkin was issued in late 1914, mostly replaced from 1915 with a hard-wearing brown leather version. Protection from the wet weather of Flanders was through an issue groundsheet, later redesigned as a rain cape.

The principal weapon of the British soldier from 1902 onwards had been the Short Magazine Lee-Enfield rifle or SMLE. Its ammunition clips or 'chargers' held five Mark VII .303 calibre bullets, the rifle magazine holding ten altogether. With the development of this short rifle came the need for a longer bayonet – 17in long. This was required as the likely enemy of the British soldier would be equipped with the longer Mauser-type rifle, meaning that he would be at a disadvantage in a lunging bayonet fight. As the war developed, the hand grenade was to replace the rifle as the primary offensive weapon of trench warfare; it required little training to use and, placed correctly, grenades had a wide kill radius that was more efficient than the well-placed shot of even the most skilled marksman.

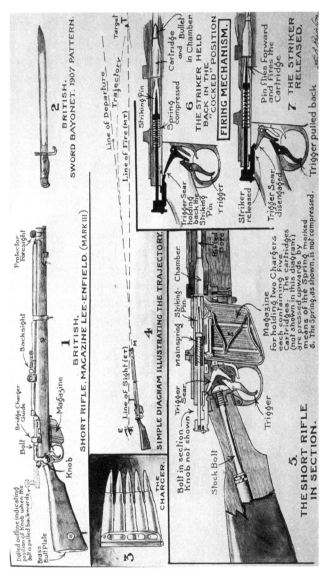

11. *The Short Magazine Lee-Enfield rifle, the principal weapon of the British infantryman.*

12. The British 'cricket-ball' grenade. This required ignition from a striker, temperamental when wet.

Grenades were certainly to have a major role in the trench fighting at Loos. The British Army went to war in 1914 with an extremely cumbersome 16in stick grenade, replaced in early 1915 by temporary solutions, the jam tin of 1915 being typical: literally a tin filled with explosive guncotton and shrapnel balls. Other short-lived types, such as the cast-iron Battye grenade, produced locally at Bethune, were also created. Both of these, plus the official cricket-ball spherical grenade, required ignition from a cardboard striker worn on the arm – this was easily put out of action in wet or damp conditions. It was with the introduction of the Mills grenade in May 1915 that the weapon was to become more successful. The secret of the Mills' success lay with its ignition system, using a spring-loaded striker, activated when a pin

13. The British 1908 pattern webbing equipment set.

was removed. This released a lever, which initiated a four-second fuse, during which time the bomber had to throw the grenade. This would see limited use at Loos, but would undoubtedly have been decisive in some of the many minor actions in the desperate fights along the fragile line there.

The 1908 webbing equipment used by the British soldier was innovative and well balanced; a complete 'system'. The set consisted of belt, cross straps, left and right cartridge carriers (designed to carry 150 rounds in ten pouches, each holding three

GRENADES

The British Army originally went to war with a long-handled percussion grenade that was all too easy to hit against the opposite side of the trench. Replacements, in number, were required: numerous locally produced or emergency grenades, mostly lit using a friction striker, which was a hit-or-miss operation. The most numerous used at Loos, two-thirds of the total available, was the spherical cricket-ball grenade; others included the hair brush, a wooden slab with guncotton attached. Mills bombs, latterly invented, were carried only by the Guards division, and in low numbers. It would become the mainstay of British trench warfare from early 1916.

five-round chargers), water bottle, entrenching tool head carrier and bayonet 'frog' (leather or canvas sheath). In addition, there was a small haversack and large pack, usually left in the rear. The equipment could be taken off like a jacket and on the march the 3in-wide belt could be unbuckled for comfort. In 1914, due to supply difficulties with the webbing equipment sets, leather versions were issued. These had distinctive, simple leather ammunition pouches, designed to take fifty cartridges each in five-round chargers – 100 rounds in all. The resulting set is most commonly seen being worn by the men of Kitchener's New Army.

Field Marshal Sir John French

Field Marshal French was the commander-in-chief of the British Expeditionary Force from 1914–15. He was a cavalry commander during the Second Boer War of 1899–1902, when he led the 1st Cavalry Brigade. After a spell as commander-in-chief of Aldershot Command, he was promoted to full general, becoming inspector general of the army during 1907–12. Promoted to field marshal in May 1913, he became Chief of the Imperial General Staff, though he resigned his post in April 1914 in the wake of the infamous Curragh Mutiny (in which officers resigned their positions rather than face up to the Ulster Volunteer Force). He was to take up the post of inspector general again, however, and was serving in this role as war threatened.

As an experienced and senior soldier, French was appointed command of the BEF in August 1914. It was French that led the BEF into its position at Mons in 1914 – against the advice of Kitchener (and Haig) who suggested a position further south – leading to an almost immediate retirement in the face of the German onslaught, its flanks failing. Famously, Sir John's orders demanded the abandonment of not only positions, but also valuable equipment; orders that were to be ignored by General Sir Horrace Smith-Dorrien, commander of the II Corps, who turned to fight at Le Cateau instead of retiring. This action was to relieve pressure on the retiring BEF – but was to lose Smith-Dorrien his job, particularly when he advocated the partial abandonment of the Belgian city of Ypres during the German offensive of April–May 1915.

Despite his name, Sir John's relationship with his French allies was fragile, being placed in the difficult role of, on the one hand, being a subordinate ally to the more numerous and substantial French, supporting General Joffre, and on the other, maintaining the independence of the BEF. Sir John was forced into political debates that he would rather have steered clear of, particularly as he was recognised as a volatile general. Nevertheless, he oversaw the difficult years of command in 1914–15, when the Allies were under pressure from the Germans, with at times unrealistic demands and inadequate resources. Faced with demands from Joffre to support the French offensives in Artois, counterpoint to the offensives in the Champagne, Sir John was inclined to take the defensive, believing that the BEF was undergunned and undermanned – at least until the arrival of Kitchener's new armies. Despite this, and

14. Field Marshal Sir John French.

ordered to support the French at all costs, Sir John participated in the battles of Neuve Chapelle (in which there was a limited breakthrough), Aubers Ridge and Festubert during 1915.

French's role at Loos was indecisive. Still holding on to the view that his armies should stand on the defensive until reinforced, he at first agreed to the battle and then shrank back from it. With this in view, it was Sir John's fateful decision to retain the XI Corps under his direct control that was to put strain on his fragile command. In reserve at Lilliers – 15 miles from the battle front – these inexperienced divisions were committed to a march that would be fraught with difficulties, and which would put intolerable strain on the commander of the First Army, Sir Douglas Haig. With failure to break through at Loos, and with French trying to gloss over the issues, Haig would push for his removal – and would find himself in Sir John's position as commander-in-chief of the BEF from December 1915. French would return to become commander-in-chief of British Home Forces in December 1915, and would oversee the British armed response to the Irish Rebellion in 1916. He would be made Lord Lieutenant of Ireland in May 1918, surviving an attempt on his life in December 1919. He died in 1925.

General Sir Douglas Haig

Sir Douglas Haig was born to a family of Scotch whisky distillers, and, unusually for generals of his day, had a university education at Oxford. He did not attain his degree due to absence from illness, but passed his exams and so was eligible for service at Sandhurst.

Sir Douglas would serve as a staff officer in the Sudan campaign of 1898, where he took part in several actions. Haig would later become assistant adjutant-general to the 1st Cavalry Brigade during the Second Boer War, 1899–1902. It would be commanded by Sir John French, and, with his superior, Haig took active part in the Siege of Ladysmith in November 1899. He would have a varied career in South Africa, part of which included a column in the Cape Colony, taking part in the suppression of the Boers. Sir Douglas returned home in 1906 as Director of Military Training on the General Staff, and took up the role of Director of Staff Duties in 1907, a role in which he supervised the publication of *Field Service Regulations*, which would be used actively during the coming war. Promoted to lieutenant general in 1910, he took up the position of General Officer Commanding, Aldershot Command in 1912, which would form the bulk of the I Corps of the BEF in August 1914.

Haig would take part in the BEF's withdrawal from Mons in 1914, with I Corps eventually taking up its position at Ypres at the end of 1914, holding the line and ensuring that the city would not be lost. In December 1914, I Corps would become the First Army, with Haig in command. The First Army took a major role in the campaigns of 1915. At Neuve Chapelle, it was Haig's army that took the offensive, supporting the synchronous French Artois and Champagne operations. Four divisions attacked on 10 March, penetrating the German lines, but were ultimately to be forced back in the absence of heavy artillery and supporting ammunition. Haig would be back in action in Artois at Aubers Ridge in May, and in a renewed offensive to the south at Festubert later that month, both with limited outcome. With Joffre still insisting that the British press the Germans in Artois, in June 1915 it was Haig who was called to survey the terrain on behalf of Sir John French, and it was he who would express dissatisfaction at the state of the ground. For Haig, more opportunity lay north of the La Bassée canal. He would be overruled, by Kitchener's desire to support the French at all costs and by French who was put in an impossible position by Joffre.

Loos was a defining moment for Haig, who committed to the battle despite his initial reservations. Rather than fighting an offensive with limited objectives in support of the French,

15. *General Sir Douglas Haig.*

who were to engage to the south of Lens, Haig, described as an 'incurable optimist' by some writers, believed he could make a decisive breakthrough. Poison gas, first used by the Germans at Ypres in April, would be his wonder weapon – standing in for the dearth of artillery that was to plague the BEF throughout 1915. The battle would see variable results, dependant in part on the terrain, upon the variability of the success of the gas 'accessory' and on the limited availability of artillery. Haig would also be challenged by a lack of reserves, a 'command and control' issue between the commander of the First Army and the commander-in-chief of the BEF, Sir John French. Held in reserve by Sir John miles from the battlefront, the XI Corps would have a torrid time getting to the front and would ultimately be broken on the strong German second defensive line. For Haig, Sir John's 'dead hand' on the reserves became a point of contention, and became a *cause celebré* in the press. With Haig having the ear of the king, it was not long before French was to be withdrawn from command, Haig himself assuming command of the BEF on 10 December 1915. He would lead the force on its 'learning curve' for the rest of the war.

Not without controversy, Haig's command has been reviewed ever since, particularly his actions on the Somme and at Third Ypres. Less discussed, until recently, has been his actions in leading his armies to decisive victory in 1918. He was made the 1st Earl Haig in March 1919 and retired from active service in April 1920. Instrumental in setting up the Haig Fund of the Royal British Legion in 1921, he died in January 1928 and received a state funeral.

The Imperial German Army

The Imperial German Army, the *Kaiserliches Heer* or *Reichsheer*, was formed in the wake of the Franco-Prussian War of 1871, and was composed of the armies of the numerous states that made up the German Empire. Dominant in this was the strong state of Prussia, which was the central part of the North German Confederation of states. The Prussian Army was to lead in all military aspects, co-ordinating matters with the other non-Confederation states of Bavaria, Württemberg and Saxony. Each possessed semi-autonomous military contingents with their own identity and customs. However, it was the Kaiser, the King of Prussia, who was the head of the army of these states – minus the Bavarian contingent, which, though co-ordinating with the Prussians, maintained its own Ministry of War and a Royal Bavarian General Staff.

In the main, though, the Kaiser exercised control though the Imperial Military Cabinet and the General Staff, the chief of which provided the main military advice. It was through the General Staff that the Prussian Army system of excellence in leadership and organisation was maintained. The Imperial German Army in peacetime was divided into eight *Armee-Inspektions* (army inspectorates), the equivalent of an army area, with the Bavarians maintaining their own independent structure. At the outbreak of war, the inspectorates formed the command structure of field armies, and by 1918 these had grown to form nineteen armies in the field. The force was further organised into *Heeresgruppe* (army groups), composed of several armies. In turn, these armies would be divided into *Armeekorps* (army corps).

The *Armeekorps* was an important formation and consisted of two or more divisions, a *Jäger* battalion, together with their support troops, artillery, engineers and logistical arms, comprising a foot artillery battalion, an engineer battalion and a logistical train battalion. The *Armeekorps* would also ensure that

Landwehr and other reserve units were organised in their areas of jurisdiction. In 1914, there would be twenty-one areas under Prussian control and a further three under Bavarian control. There was also an elite Prussian *Gardekorps* (guard corps).

In common with the British Army, in the German Army the division was a basic tactical formation; but unlike those of their enemies, the standard German division comprised just two brigades (each with two infantry regiments), together with cavalry and artillery brigades. The cavalry were later to be given up, to form separate cavalry divisions, and engineers would be drafted in from the corps. At the outbreak of war there would be forty-two regular divisions in the Prussian Army (including four Saxon divisions and two Württemberg divisions), as well as six divisions contributed by the semi-independent Bavarian Army. All would be mobilised for war, and there were additional troops in the form of *Landwehr*, consisting of soldiers that had completed their formal period of engagement with the regular forces. The *Landwehr* brigades were organised into divisions, and there would be *ersatz* or replacement units made from home guard (*Landsturm*). By the end of the war 251 divisions had been formed in the German Army.

With two per brigade, the regiment was the basic home of the German soldier, actively recruiting and training its men, and there were infantry, cavalry and artillery regiments. Each infantry regiment was composed of three battalions and, unlike the British, each of these battalions would serve together – British battalions would be distributed to separate brigades, most often to separate divisions. As such, German regiments were broadly equivalent to British brigades. *Landwehr* regiments were added during the war, called up from the trained reserves. *Landsturm* battalions consisted of men either too young to join a regular regiment or too old to be recalled to the *Landwehr*. Specialists such as the *Pionere* (engineers) and signals troops were formed into smaller effective units. *Jäger* battalions were light infantrymen, with a range of weapons and tactical skills.

16. *German soldier dressed in* Waffenrock *jacket with Saxon cuffs, and with the* Pickelhaube *in its cover. He is fully equipped and carries the 1898 pattern rifle.*

German Army Uniforms and Equipment

German soldiers were equipped with a field-grey (*Feldgrau*) service uniform that had been introduced in 1910. It comprised a single-breasted uniform jacket, the *Waffenrock*, which was worn by both infantry and cavalry alike. *Jägers* wore it too, but in a grey-green (*Graugrün*) version. The *Waffenrock* was a loose-fitting garment with stand and fall collar (sometimes with collar bars, or *Litzen*, denoting regimental seniority), two pockets with buttoned flaps in the skirts, and with eight simple tombak or nickel buttons to fasten it, bearing either a crown or a lion (identifying Bavarian troops). Shoulder straps bore the regimental number in colours denoting arm of service – red for infantry or green for *Jäger*, for instance – and these colours were piped around the edge of the uniform jacket as well. Shoulder straps were piped with colours that indicated the *Armeekorps* in the infantry. The *Waffenrock* jacket was further distinguished by differences in the cuffs, with four main types: Brandenburg, Swedish, Saxon and French – fashions adopted by some regiments and varying in the style of turnback and arrangement of decorative buttons. These distinctions started to be shed as the war deepened, and in September 1915 this jacket was replaced by a simpler *Bluse*, with concealed buttons. Both jackets were worn with trousers (*Tuchhose*) piped with the arm of service, but again different patterns (including corduroy trousers, which emerged during the war), tucked into the distinctive black leather knee boots – although low boots and puttees would start to appear as the war progressed.

In common with the practice in most armies, the German officer typically wore a personally tailored version of the standard uniform. This ensured that the officer was well dressed and distinctive, though perhaps less so that his British opposite number, who was easily picked out by snipers. With *Waffenrock* well fitted, officers would also wear better-quality headgear, as

17. German officers standing in a communication trench, pictured in 1915. Both wear the Bluse.

well as breeches – often with exaggerated form – and better-fitting boots. Officers would wear belts and be equipped with a range of semi-automatic pistols, including the famous pre-war 'broomhandle' Mauser.

The most distinctive of all uniform items – highly prized by the British soldier as a souvenir item – would be the spiked helmet,

18. The 1915 pattern Pickelhaube, with subdued grey metal fittings.

or *Pickelhaube*. The *Pickelhaube* was first adopted by German troops in 1842, and was worn throughout the remainder of the nineteenth century into the First World War. The pattern used in the war was first issued in 1895 and consisted of a leather body with brass fittings and spikes (or ball fitting for artillery). The various state armies were distinguished by the individual design of their helmet plates (*Wappen*). The complex *Pickelhaube* would be simplified and constructed from replacement materials as the war dragged on. In 1915, the *Pickelhaube* was simplified with grey-painted steel fittings. To hide its reflective surfaces, the helmet was worn with a rush-green or field-grey cover, which was marked with the regimental number in green (red in 1914). From September 1915, the helmet was worn without its spike at the front, and was to be universally replaced in 1916 by the steel *Stalhelm* helmet. Other arms, such as the *Jägers* and *Landsturm*,

19. German Landsturm soldier, with distinctive cap.

wore different headgear, with *Jägers* wearing simple shakos. Out of the line, the 'pork pie', peak-less *Feldmütze* cap, much derided in British propaganda images of German soldiers, was worn. *Landsturm* men wore taller caps, with distinctive cross badges.

The German infantryman was supplied with a brown leather equipment set of 1909 pattern, consisting of three ammunition pouches on a belt bearing a brass and nickel buckle. This buckle varied according to state origin, but commonly bore the legend *Gott mit Uns* (God with us) and the Prussian crown. The weight of the ammunition on the belt was supported by shoulder straps that joined in the centre of the back in the shape of a Y. In full equipment, the German soldier carried a distinctive hide-covered (later just canvas) field pack on his shoulders, his field-grey greatcoat worn rolled and attached to the top of the pack. Personal equipment was finished off with a flask-shaped water bottle, a fabric 'bread bag' (*Brotheutal*, which held the soldier's daily ration and spare rounds of ammunition) and a bayonet in its frog over a shovel-shaped entrenching tool, all suspended from the belt. The bayonet varied in size and form; the notorious 'butcher bayonet' was a saw-backed tool issued to *Pionere*.

The principal weapon of the German infantryman was the *Gewehr* 1898 pattern 7.9mm Mauser rifle, which had a five-round magazine, and he could also field the formidable 'potato masher' stick grenade, which was armed by pulling a toggle before release. The potato masher could be launched a long distance. Other grenades, such as the pre-war pattern segmented *Kugelhandgrenate* and disc-like *Diskushandgrenate*, were also in evidence at Loos.

General Bertram Sixt von Armin

Like his contemporaries, Sixt von Armin had served in the last major conflict with France, during the Franco–Prussian War of 1870–71. As a cadet in the 4th Grenadier Guards, he was wounded at the Battle of Gravelotte in 1870, in which the Prussian victors lost four times more men than their French opponents. Decorated with the Iron Cross First Class, von Armin would then rise to serve as the adjutant of his regiment. His military career was to take off during the early part of the twentieth century. Promoted to the command of the *55. Regiment* as *Oberst*, he rose quickly to become the Chief of Staff of the *Gardekorps* of the Royal Prussian Army, comprising the 1st and 2nd *Garde-Infanterie-Divisions* and the *Garde-Kavallerie-Division*. Promoted to major general in 1903, he rose to lieutenant general in 1906.

After a spell in charge of the *13. Division*, Sixt von Armin succeeded von Hindenburg to command the *IV Armeekorps* and in 1913 he achieved the rank of general. At the outbreak of war, the *IV Armeekorps* formed part of the *6. Armee*, commanded by Kronprinz Rupprecht von Bayern, and took an active part

in the Battle of Lorraine, holding the line against the prosecution of the French Plan XVII, the invasion of Alsace-Lorraine, in August 1914. The *6. Armee* would later move to northern France. It was the *6. Armee* and the *IV Armeekorps*, commanded by von Armin who would repel the attacks by Joffre and Sir John French in the Noyon Salient.

20. General Bertram Sixt von Armin.

Von Armin would distinguish himself later in the war and would be awarded the *Pour le Mérite*, the highest German honour, in 1916; in 1917 he would be promoted to the command of the *4. Armee* in Flanders. He would be further decorated for his defence of the German lines in the face of British assaults at Third Ypres. At the end of the war, Sixt von Armin commanded *Heeresgruppe A*, returning with his command to Germany, where he resigned from military command. He died in 1936 and was buried with full military honours.

THE DAYS
BEFORE BATTLE

It was a hideous territory, this Black Country between Lens and Hulluch. From the flat country below the distant ridges of Notre Dame de Lorette and Vimy there rose a number of high, black cones made by the refuse of the coal mines, which were called Fosses. Around those black mounds there was great slaughter.

Philip Gibbs, 1933

The Loos battlefield lies between the canal at La Bassée and the Lens–Noeux-les-Mines railway. Loos itself – now known as Loos-en-Gohelle – was a mining village surrounded by many other mining communities that were dotted about in this part of French Flanders, many of them small and insubstantial. Despite this, these villages and hamlets went by the title Cité, as if to emphasise their insignificance. One contemporary account gives a none-too-promising view of the landscape:

The scene of the coming conflict east of our front was not a picturesque one. It was the Black Country of France, and the open plain was dotted with squalid little red brick villages and ugly mine works, the German trenches telling out very white in the chalky soil among the conical slag-heaps and winding roads.

Newman Flower, 1916

21. The post-industrial landscape of the Loos battlefield. The remodelled Double Crassier from the position of the Lens Road Redoubt, now 'Dud Corner' CWGC cemetery.

Topographically, the Loos battlefield has been described as flat; but in fact the ground conditions were variable across the front assigned to the British for the coming offensive. The ground is chalky (a condition familiar to those British regiments hailing from southern counties), yet the slagheaps and pitheads (*fosses*, together with shafts, or *puits*) and the huge, glowering piles of dark, non-reflective colliery wastes – known as crassiers – give evidence to the once feverish mining activity below ground. Clustered around these works were miners' cottages known as *corons*.

Once one of the most important coal mining regions of France, here the mines go deep underground, beneath a thick chalk layer that creates the low rolling profile of the landscape, more akin to the downs of southern England – though scarred as if in the coalfields of more northerly counties. To the south of Loos, the chalk grounds are thrust upwards to create the upland of the Artois plateau, which has as its northern margin a large natural break or fault that both lifted Vimy Ridge and the upland of Notre Dame de Lorette and depressed the wet Flanders plain north of Lens. It is the discordance between pastoral chalk landscape and industrial wasteland that helps define this region like no other.

The natural landscape varies from the south to the north, with the British and German lines trending pretty much north–south across the region in a lazy arc, deliberately sited to give maximum natural support to the trench fortifications that had been dug there – and feverishly upgraded in July 1915 by the Germans, in some cases with the use of French labour. In the Ypres Salient to the north, the Germans had the advantage of the high ground, but also had the topographical inconvenience of wet, water-bearing ground layers that caused them to rely upon surface concrete fortifications that would come to be known as pillboxes. For the British, in the porous chalky layers of French Flanders, the ground would be drier, surface water draining away through the chalk to join both La Bassée canal to the north and the canal de Lens to the south. In the sector closest to Lens, and to the Artois plateau itself, the ground has a rolling aspect, the village of Loos nesting in a low valley between two lazy spurs – one at Grenay, the other from Lens. To the north, the ground flattens out and becomes open, windswept and desolate, as well as much flatter.

Though surfaced with a rich soil, it did not take much to dig down to the loose, broken chalk that would be easy to create deep trenches in and, even more importantly, deep dugouts that would be proof from the searching attentions of any howitzer shells that might be available to the attackers. This situation was prescient of another 'big push', in July 1916, when British and

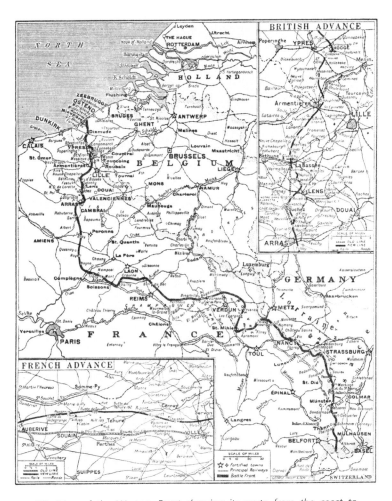

22. Map of the Western Front showing its route from the coast to the Swiss frontier, with insets showing the position of Artois and the Champagne.

French troops attacked in similar ground on the Somme. On his arrival at Loos after the main battles were fought, James Norman Hall observed the strength of the German defences:

Under a clayish surface soil there was a stratum of solid chalk. Advantage of this had been taken by the German engineers who must have planned and supervisd the work. Many of the shell-proof dugouts were fifteen and even twenty feet below the surface of the ground. Stairways just large enough to permit the passage of a man's body led down to them. The roofs were reinforced with heavy timbers.

Pte James Norman Hall, 9th Royal Fusiliers

In being assigned to this sector, the British attackers would have to face two lines of strongly dug trenches, with deep dugouts. With knowledge of Anglo-French intentions, the Germans had greatly strengthened their defences in situ, with a chain of mutually supporting strongpoints (*stutzpunkts*), some of which would be significant redoubts or forts. Two of the most infamous would be the Hohenzollern Redoubt in the north, between Haisnes and Hulluch, backed by the observation point of *Fosse 8*, a tall slagheap; and Hill 70 in the south, a natural feature forming the backdrop to the village of Loos, itself defended by linked strongpoints. In front of this was the most significant of all pithead gear, the startlingly elegant yet terribly open framework dubbed by the British troops 'Tower Bridge'. There would be numerous other strongpoints and redoubts in the German frontline, and even more in the second line that had been constructed during the summer of 1915, roughly paralleling the Lens–La Bassée road. Here the line comprised strongpoints at regular intervals, sweeping around on contours to enfilade attackers skilfully, supported by deep trenches and thickly spread barbed-wire thickets.

For Sir Douglas Haig, commanding the First Army, the terrain was not just unattractive; it represented a distinctly tough nut to crack. In June 1915, Sir John French dispatched Haig to make an appreciation of the ground in order to consider whether the demands of Joffre and his able lieutenant, Foch, were something

23. 'Tower Bridge', the pithead gear from Puits 15, in Loos.

that could be realistically delivered by the British. Haig was not confident. The miners' cottages and slagheaps provided the Germans with numerous opportunities for active observation and spirited defence; between the industrial paraphernalia was an agricultural landscape that was largely barren of trees and open in aspect. In his report to Sir John French, Haig concluded that the ground was not favourable to attack:

> The ground, for the most part bare and open, would be so swept by machine-gun and rifle fire both from the German front trenches and the numerous fortified villages immediately behind them that a rapid advance would be impossible.
>
> General Sir Douglas Haig

In fact, he went on:

> The German defences were so strong that until a greatly increased establishment of heavy artillery was provided, that they could only be taken by siege methods; that is by a series of progressive attacks from trench to trench which would involve hand-to-hand fighting and bombing.
>
> General Sir Douglas Haig

Haig's opinions were to be borne out by future events. Instead of attacking here, he was of the opinion that any assault should instead be delivered north of La Bassée canal, in a region that had already been fought over in the three abortive offensives carried out by the BEF so far in 1915 – particularly in the light of the increased defensive capability of the German second line. He also entertained the possibility of moving troops to the south of Arras and supporting the French Tenth Army in this position. A third option was to return to the Ypres Salient and attack the Messines–Wytschaete Salient – a suggestion unrealistic in delivering the aim of supporting the Tenth Army in its distant assault in Artois. Armed with these opinions, Sir John French sought a conference with General Foch, the architect of the attacks in Artois and commander of the northern group of armies. Foch's answer was firm: that a British attack south of La Bassée canal was of paramount importance in support of the French, if only to draw off and counter the fire of enemy artillery along the whole of the front. The attack would have to stand. His chief, Joffre, would reiterate his support of the region – a view diametrically opposed to that of Haig:

It seems to me that no more favourable ground than that which extends from the north of Angres to the La Bassée canal can be found on which to carry out the general offensive of the British Army … I cannot suggest a better direction of attack than the line Loos–Hulluch and the ground extending to the La Bassée canal, with the final objective Hill 70 and Pont à Vendin.

General Joseph Joffre

In the face of this unequivocal view, Sir John tried meekly to restrict the British involvement to an artillery battle alone; it fell on deaf ears. Thus in August 1915 it was the worsening situation on other fronts that was to force his hand. The Italians, newcomers to the European war, were facing defeat against the Austrians on the Isonzo River, two offensives having already failed, and Sir Ian Hamilton's efforts to break the stalemate in Gallipoli had stagnated. However, it was the fact that the Russians were under severe pressure on the Eastern Front, their lines contracting so much so as to force the abandonment of Poland, which created the greatest alarm. If the Russians were to collapse, then the transference of some sixty-plus divisions westwards could be decisive. It was imperative that there was an attack eastwards. The Secretary of State for War, Field Marshal Lord Kitchener, instructed Sir John French accordingly: 'we must act with all our energy and do our utmost to help France in their offensive, even though in so doing we may suffer very heavy losses.' The die was cast. Sir John informed Joffre that the First Army would attack 'with all its resources' south of La Bassée canal. The Germans expected as much:

In front of the blue-black slagheap on the right of Loos they placed a large white board with the question written fair in big, black letters: 'WHEN IS THE BIG PUSH COMING OFF? WE ARE WAITING.'

Patrick MacGill, 1/18th London Regiment

Sir John French issued his orders for the 'big push' on 18 September 1915. It would be fought between Lens and La Bassée, and was to be conducted by Haig, his First Army carrying out the main assault. Two Corps, IV and I, were to spearhead the assault; north of the canal there would be subsidiary attacks in order to draw out the German defenders made by the III Corps and the Indian Corps. There would be other evidence of British and Commonwealth assistance; to the north, in the Ypres Salient, there would be attacks against Hooge, on the Menin road, and at Messines, intended to confuse the Germans as to British intentions. Also, farther to the south, the Third Army now in position on the Somme was to deploy its artillery in support of the southern flanks of the French Tenth Army assault. However, it was Sir John's decision to retain personal control of the XI Corps, together with the Cavalry Corps and the Indian Cavalry Corps, as a strong reserve that was to create one of the greatest controversies of the battle – and was ultimately to provide the leverage that would see him ousted from his position as commander-in-chief by the end of the year.

The XI Corps was a composite: it had regulars, the Guards Division; Territorials, in the shape of the 46th (North Midland) Division; and men of Kitchener's army, the 12th (Eastern) Division (of K1 vintage, the 'First Hundred Thousand') and two particularly raw and untried K3 (Third Hundred Thousand) divisions, the 21st (raised in Tring of mostly north country men) and 24th (formed in Shoreham in Sussex, with men from the eastern counties). These last two divisions would land in France in early September and would find themselves thrust into battle with almost no acclimatisation. This would prove to be a costly mistake, and would be the central bone of contention in the post-battle recriminations.

To the I Corps (commanded by Lieutenant General Hubert Gough) was allotted the task of taking the position from just north of La Bassée canal to the Hulluch–Vermelles road. It would

24. 'Big' and 'Little Willie' – irreverent names for the Kaiser and his son – and the names of the linking trenches of the Hohenzollern Redoubt.

face the considerable fortifications of the German first line, with the works known as the Hohenzollern Redoubt – consisting of entrenchments and deep dugouts – a major hazard to the hoped for result. The redoubt itself thrust forwards towards the British lines, defiantly, and was connected to major trench works, 'Big' and 'Little Willie', irreverent British nicknames for the Kaiser and his Crown Prince son. Behind was the slagheap of *Fosse 8*, which the Germans had fortified and equipped as an efficient observation base. The surrounding miners' villages had also been turned into considerable fortifications, as had the chalk quarries in the vicinity of Hulluch.

South of the Hulluch–Vermelles road, the frontage was allotted to the IV Corps (commanded by Lieutenant General Sir Henry Rawlinson). Here the line swung round over the disputed 'unfavourable' ground before approaching the outskirts of the village of Loos, and the long, dark mass of the Double Crassier, a double-lined, linear slagheap (now piled up into great black cones) that seemed to soak up the light around it. Behind the streets of the village, still occupied by some brave (or foolish) civilians, was the mass of another slagheap, the Loos Crassier; close by was the strangely beautiful open-boxwork, twin-pylon winding gear of the deep mines below. The London troops facing it were to christen this 'Tower Bridge'; the Germans overlooking the British below knew that they were safe from the ineffective fire of the British artillery (the works would not be destroyed by British artillery fire).

The battle was to open with a preliminary bombardment at 7am on 21 September 1915. If Neuve Chapelle, still in the minds of the British commanders, had taught them anything, it was the need for accurate and heavy artillery fire. Yet, with the numbers of guns, howitzers and ammunition in short supply to the British – unlike those available to their French allies – maintaining a significant, pre-battle bombardment of the heavily entrenched enemy positions was going to be a major issue. This was particularly the case as the length of artillery frontage at Loos had increased tenfold over that at Neuve Chapelle earlier in the year. Yet the total number of artillery pieces had increased to 871, just 336 more than had been used in the earlier battle,

AMERICAN 3-INCH   RUSSIAN 3-INCH   GERMAN 77 M.M. (3.05")   FRENCH 75 M.M. (2.95")   BRITISH 18 POUNDER 3.29")

25. Shrapnel shells. The British 18-pounder shell (right) was deployed to cut barbed wire, with variable results.

but on a much narrower front. Of these, 594 were flat-trajectory field guns, shown to be of limited effectiveness in trench warfare and requiring great skill in removing the threat of barbed wire by active cutting with low-bursting shrapnel. On the day, this aim would not always be achieved.

Mustering all the guns and howitzers that could be spared, artillery shells had also been husbanded to provide a fighting chance of destroying the enemy positions. As one recent commentator, Jonathan Bailey, has put it: 'artillery required unprecedented supplies of ammunition if it was to win the firefight … [and] by the end of 1915, it had been determined that the committal of infantry to the attack without a certain number of rounds per metre of front would result in failure.' This would certainly ring true at Loos. Hopes were high, however, that the lessons of Neuve Chapelle had been well learned. Despite this, and with the increased battle frontage, there was in fact to be only one artillery piece per 23yds, one-fifth of what was available at the earlier battle. With fewer weapons came the need for a much longer preliminary bombardment, thereby sacrificing surprise. The ideal of the 'hurricane' bombardment, with a dramatic weight of shells launched against both positions and men in a short space of time, thereby creating maximum confusion and potential for surprise destruction, would have to await the output of Britain's reorganised munitions industries and would be a key feature of the more successful British endeavours of 1917–18.

With 300 rounds per field gun being available in early 1915 (three times the number of 1914), recent analysis suggests that this had been increased dramatically in time for Loos; but even this would be inadequate given the much-increased frontage. Though field guns were equipped with more ammunition than had been available to the artillery in the earlier battles, even the suggested 1,000 rounds per field gun and 400 rounds per howitzer would be insufficient to silence the German defenders, flatten their defences and reduce their wire to dust.

British inadequacy in the weight of munitions available was compounded by the unreliability of the shells themselves. As indicated by the ironic choice of name for the main British memorial to the battle, Dud Corner, the 1,000 rounds available could only be nominal; there would be many misfires from worn artillery pieces and, as at the Somme in 1916, as many as 30 per cent of the shells sourced from commercial suppliers would fail to explode or would shed their drivebands on leaving the gun barrel, thereby causing the shells to veer off target. Also, with the majority of the guns available to the British being the reliable but flat-trajectory 18-pounder field gun, the opportunity to destroy deep dugouts was limited, particularly as shrapnel shells were the commonest rounds supplied to the guns. Effective anti-personnel weapons, these shells delivered around 240 round lead balls from air bursts set by timer fuses, yet were pretty much useless against the deep, hard chalk dugouts of the enemy they were hoping to destroy. Wire cutting was another matter, though shrapnel could be effective if they could be delivered efficiently, close to the entanglements.

At this time in the war the science of counter-battery fire was limited and the concentration of effort was the thick wire in front of the fire trenches and the deep trenches themselves. Less than 10 per cent of the artillery effort would be focused against the enemy guns, the very weapons that would themselves come into action against the advancing British soldiers on 25 September 1915. In any case, gunnery was yet to build in the high scientific flourishes that would see howitzers fire against long-distance, unsighted targets. At Loos this would have great significance. Though parts of the battle front were pretty open, in other areas the rolling contours derived from the slopes of the Artois plateau meant that the howitzer batteries of the RFA were placed on reverse slopes, situated some 3,000–4,000yds away from their targets. The clutter and industrial detritus of the mines was also a major factor in crowding the landscape, even though in places the enemy lines could be clearly picked out in bright white chalk lines across the dull industrial-pastoral landscape. None of this was helped by the fact that during the bombardment observation of fire accuracy was difficult, clouded by chalk dust and mists that spread across the battle front. It would be the responsibility of forward observation officers to watch the shells fly overhead to their respective targets:

Up at the observation post ... the observing officer sits,
watching the black and yellow smoke clouds of the bursting
high explosive, or the cotton-wool-like puffs of the shrapnel.
The words of the telephonists seem to come from a different
world. Here she comes, far away behind, the whistle of the
shell shrieking louder as she passes right overhead – splendid!

Major C.J.C. Street RFA

To tempt the Germans into their trenches – thereby bringing them
into positions under fire – the British laid on a number of ruses, called
'Chinese attacks' (a probable hangover from the Boxer Rebellion),
at a time that it was hoped would add to the effectiveness of the
bombardment. On each of its four days, units in the frontline
trenches were detailed to stand-to and fire two minutes of rapid fire
with rifles and machine-guns; bayonets were brandished above the
parapets, there were shouts and bagpipes or bugles sounded. Even
head and shoulders dummies, fashioned by the Pioneer battalions,
were shown as potential targets above the parapet. These ruses
worked here and there along the line, when the 18-pounders were
able to sight their targets over open sights. This feint would be
retried just before zero hour on the 25th – here, the dummies would
reappear in no-man's-land, having been dragged through shallow
Russian saps (a trench built at right angles to the frontline) unseen.

The inadequacies of the artillery bombardment were well
appreciated by General Haig in advance of the attack. Though
there were more guns and ammunition, given previous
experience, for all its best intentions, the weight of fire mustered
by the RFA must surely still be inadequate. Haig's grasp of the
situation was that the use of gas would effectively make up for
the deficiencies, with the estimate that the planned gas attack
could double the effectiveness of the guns. Sir Douglas Haig
was quick to seize the opportunity of this weapon following its
deployment by the Germans farther to the north at Ypres. With
Kitchener's orders clear – that the British should seek to retaliate

and to develop gas capability and assets – and with the effective demonstration of this capability, Haig was convinced. However, as Jonathan Bailey has suggested, this would be 'an expectation that was badly disappointed when the wind failed to cooperate with the gas'.

Haig's plan to use poison gas was necessarily predicated on satisfactory wind conditions, and elaborate precautions were put in place in order to make sure that the gas cloud would form and would then roll over the ground towards the German trenches. As chlorine gas is heavier than air, it was expected that a breeze would be sufficient to drive the gas towards the German lines, the cloud effectively hugging its contours, sinking into trenches and dugouts. Given the frontage, it would be essential for the gas to be released over a significant time frame – sufficient time, in fact, to overcome the usefulness of the German respirators, which were thought to protect for only thirty minutes' exposure. If the gas could overcome this, then the German troops themselves would be overcome in turn; the British would be able to walk through the line, their defenders dead or dying, if they had not already run away. At least, that was the plan. With gas replacing the effect of heavy artillery, then it was essential that a sufficiently deadly cloud could be produced to silence the enemy. The wind would have to be favourable, blowing from the west, if the heavier-than-air gas was not to hang around at its point of release.

As luck would have it, the conditions on 15 September 1915, the original date for the attack, were 'near perfect', with a strong breeze of 4mph blowing eastwards. However, as the attacks would necessarily be in concert with those of the French (and as the French attacks were not predicated on the use of gas), it was agreed with Joffre and Foch that the attacks would proceed together on 25 September. With General Haig unequivocal in his plans for the use of gas, he nevertheless built in options that allowed for three separate circumstances based on wind conditions. The first assumed optimum conditions, under which the attack would proceed. The second, with limited wind, allowed for a partial assault of the 9th Division (I Corps) against the Hohenzollern Redoubt and the 15th Division (IV Corps) to the north of Loos, to be followed up with a complete attack a day later; the third option was similar to the second, but allowed for a further delay. Neither of these latter options would have proven satisfactory in the heat of modern warfare; optimum or not, the attack would proceed.

At zero hour, the artillery bombardment lifted and the gas released:

> At forty minutes past zero, or 6.30am, every battery lifts its fire from the front line to the second line, and still the furious fire continues. And then suddenly came time zero, bringing with it a scene that could never be forgotten. From the whole length of our front trench, as far as the eye could reach, rose, vertically at first, a grey could of smoke and gas, that, impelled by a gentle wind, spread slowly towards the enemy's trenches.
>
> Major C.J.C. Street RFA

Planning for Gas

Poison gas was to be used by the British for the first time in history at the Battle of Loos. The seeds of its use were laid during its first use by the Germans in the Second Battle of Ypres in April–May 1915. Lord Kitchener, Secretary of State for War, gave instructions that retaliatory measures be prepared to use this weapon against the Germans themselves. Kitchener directed Colonel Louis Jackson of the Royal Engineers to examine the possibilities on 3 May 1915, and almost exactly a month later Jackson and his team, including academic and industrial chemists from the Kestner-Kellner Alkali Company, carried out a large-scale trial of the release of chlorine gas from cylinders in the chemical factories of Runcorn. Though the Germans used a mixture of chlorine and bromine in their attack, it was only chlorine that could be produced in sufficient quantities, with 10 tons of the gas being produced a day from an initial starting point of 2 or 3 tons.

During the Runcorn test, carried out on 4 June 1915, came the means of delivering the gas from cylinders, at the suggestion of Major C.H. Foulkes RE, the future commander of the 'Special Companies', as the Royal Engineers given the responsibility of handling the gas were to be called. This would be the last major test of gas release before zero hour on 25 September 1915, though Haig would see a limited demonstration of the formation of a 'chlorine wave' at Helfaut in France, on 22 August. At this point, the commander of the First Army was sufficiently impressed to make gas a central plank of his plan, which, in his words, would see gas 'lavishly employed on the whole front of attack'. It was estimated that moderate winds would be essential to form a continuous gas cloud from cylinders placed in the frontline, separated at a distance of 25yds apart. With gas cylinders sent to the front on 10 July, each was to be manhandled into position by two men.

The 'Accessory' and the 'Special Companies'

The chlorine gas – code-named 'the accessory' for secrecy – that was to be used in the assault was to be the responsibility of the 'Special Companies' of the Royal Engineers, under the enthusiastic leadership of Major, later Lieutenant Colonel, C.H. Foulkes RE. The original Special Companies were formed in Helfaut, south-east of St Omer, in July 1915, from men with specialist experience transferred from the infantry, and new companies were added right into September. Those men with suitable experience – often

26. British gas cylinders in position.

chemistry graduates – were given the rank Chemist Corporal. The Special Companies were distinguished by their multiple vertically striped pink, white and green armbands or brassards – indicating their authority to stay in the trenches during the assault. The gas was to be dispensed from cylinders fitted with flexible pipes that connected to the business end of the affair, a half-inch iron pipe that was up to 10ft long and which was fitted with a jet at its end. The chlorine was released by the Special Company personnel on being given the order to proceed, through the simple act of turning on a stopcock.

The gas cylinders were to be installed beneath the firestep in special bays of the frontline trench. There were to be just over 5,000 cylinders deployed along the British front: 2,568 for the I Corps, 2,460 for IV Corps. With working parties comprising three men to a cylinder and a deadweight to be carried in darkness along narrow communication trenches over an average distance of 1.5 miles, this meant that 8,000 men in all were deployed in getting 'the accessory' to its designated start point. Even with this great number, there were still not enough to provide a gas supply that would be continuous over a period of forty minutes – the time required to overcome the thirty minutes of estimated useful life of a German respirator. The deficiency would have to be made up with phosphorous 'smoke candles', which would ensure that the cloud was thick, the expectation being that the German defenders would have no way of telling gas from smoke. Gas would be emitted in twelve-minute bursts, with a gap of eight minutes of smoke, adding up to forty minutes of preparation. Smoke would also be delivered from 3in Stokes mortars, invented in January 1915.

Gas Masks and Hoods

Following the German gas attack in April–May, the British had come a long way from their quickly extemporised cloths soaked in alkaline solutions, such as bicarbonate of soda or even urine. Leading chemists quickly identified that a mixture of sodium hyposulphite ('hypo' as used in photographic processing), sodium carbonate and glycerine was considered proof against chlorine, bromine, sulphur dioxide and other fumes, these chemical salts neutralising the poisons, and the first issue masks were made of black mourning veil material and cotton wadding dipped in a solution of the chemicals. The mask was proven to be inadequate by scientists serving as soldiers in the BEF. One of them, Captain Cluny Macpherson, suggested a flannel bag soaked in the same solution that covered the head and was tucked into the top of the uniform jacket; it was equipped with a mica window. Macpherson's Hypo Helmet (officially, Smoke Helmet) would be issued in early May, but it would take some time for it to replace the veiling mask. There were still fears that the Hypo Helmet would not be proof against the more lethal gasses, such as phosgene or hydrogen cyanide, and as such, it was to be replaced by a new pattern, the 'P'

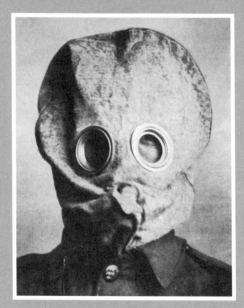

27. The nightmarish British 'P' Helmet.

28. German medic equipped with both pad respirator and Selbstretter re-breathing apparatus.

or Phenate Helmet, soaked in another counter-gas chemical, sodium phenate. The 'P' Helmet was made of cotton flannelette, the mica eyepiece replaced by circular glass eyepieces, and fitted with an outlet valve with a tube to be gripped in the mouth. At Loos, British soldiers wore both Hypo and 'P' helmets, and were supposed to carry a spare. Both were dank, stuffy and uncomfortable to wear. In the heat of the moment, men were prepared to risk being gassed than suffocated. In most cases, this would be a costly mistake. The 'P' Helmet would go through two further improvements before it was finally replaced.

Though they were first to release gas, the Germans were behind in many respects in anti-gas protection. Though the engineers in charge of gas release at Ypres were well protected, wearing the *Selbstretter* oxygen re-breathing apparatus, the infantry had to make do with locally made pads soaked in sodium hyposulphite that tied around the face with tapes. The pads were replaced in August–September 1915 by a more effective shaped mask, again to be tied around the face. This mask, the *Atemschützer*, was supplied with a metal nose clip and a glass bottle of the counter-gas solution. The troops at Loos were variously equipped; some specialists and officers had access to the re-breathing apparatus, while most in the frontline wore the hyposulphite-soaked pads tied around their faces, and others had to make do with improvised pads, again soaked in gas-countering chemicals.

THE BATTLEFIELD:
WHAT ACTUALLY HAPPENED?

I stood on the slagheap staring at this curtain of smoke hour after hour, dazed by the tumult of noise and by that impenetrable veil which hid all the human drama. The guns went on pounding away day after day – labouring, pummelling, hammering.

Philip Gibbs, 1933

21–24 September 1915

 7am   Preliminary bombardment opens on the Loos battle front, continuing until 24 September

With the battlefield bisected by the Vermelles–Hulluch road, and flanked by La Bassée canal in the north and the Lens railway in the south, the attacks opened on a bright day at zero hour, 6.30am. The bombardment that had continued for four days suddenly fell silent. It was up to the gas to do its job, released forty minutes earlier, and intended to stupefy the enemy.

However, the question of whether gas would be able to achieve what was expected of it literally hung in the air, particularly given the possibility that atmospheric conditions might not match the aspirations of Sir Douglas Haig. If the gas cloud was to form, and

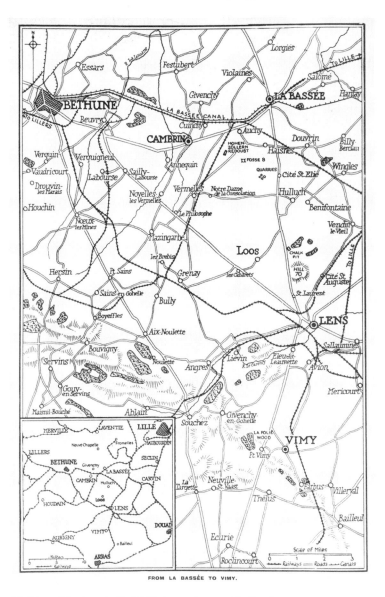

29. Map of the Loos battlefield between Lens and La Bassée.

was to roll across no-man's-land with sufficient haste, then wind would be needed, and a steady breeze of 6–8 miles an hour at the very least. Sir Douglas Haig deployed a team of meteorological experts who would be in a position to advise, from Captain E. Gold of the Royal Flying Corps, who received bulletins from the Meteorological Office in London and its equivalent in Paris, to a team of forty gas officers, who were specially trained in wind speed and direction estimation. On their shoulders was the responsibility of advising the GOC First Army; if all was not well, then the attack would stutter. Gas was the central component of Haig's plan, without it the feeble artillery bombardment would have limited effect. The wind had to be right.

On 24 September, Haig and his corps commanders met with Gold. There was no chance of a favourable wind that day; but there was the possibility that there would be a breath of wind blowing from the west the following day. Haig grasped the opportunity: 'The weather forecast … indicates that a west or south-west wind might be anticipated tomorrow, 25th September. All orders issued for the attack with gas will therefore hold good.' Nevertheless, there was the possibility that the forecast could be wrong. With the assault timed to start at 6.30am, and the gas release at 5.50am, Haig and his staff were

FAIL-SAFES

Though Haig was committed to the use of gas, every precaution had been made to stop the release, if conditions or if the local environment were to change. There were telephone links, telegraphs and dispatch riders for higher commands. There were runners ready to pass on details to gas officers. Each of these officers also had typewritten slips of paper bearing the message: 'attack postponed, taps NOT to be turned on until further notice.' Foulkes had also provided his officers with the authority not to turn on the gas if local conditions were difficult.

understandably nervous when at 5am there was hardly a breath of wind. Then, when his senior aide-de-camp, Major Fletcher, lit a cigarette, the puffs of smoke were seen to drift in exactly the opposite direction. For an expert opinion, Haig consulted with his gas officer, Lieutenant Colonel Foulkes, who confirmed that his men would not turn on the gas taps if there was a chance of the gas hanging close to the British trenches; that coupled with the fact that the breeze picked up from the south-west convinced Haig to commit to action:

> Zero hour arrived at last at 5.50am, and with a redoubled artillery bombardment the gas and smoke were released all along the front … the gas cloud was rolling steadily over towards the German lines … apart from the artillery drum-fire and the clouds of gas and smoke from eleven thousand candles, twenty-five thousand phosphorous hand-grenades were spurting out dense white fumes.
>
> Lt Col C.H. Foulkes, Commanding RE Special Companies

The effect on the Germans was, nevertheless, variable:

> The effect of the gas on our men, who were warned in time and who were able to put on their protective outfits, varied with density and the susceptibility of individuals. The smoke allowed some companies to be surprised … the masks then in use broke down under later waves. The formation of rust on the metal parts of the weapons, which had not been observed hitherto, made the guns and machine-guns useless.
>
> War Diary, *6. Armee*

25 September 1915: Opening day of the Battle of Loos

5.50am		Artillery bombardment of the German trenches along the battle front, in tandem with chlorine gas release

25 September 1915: IV Corps

Attack on the frontage between Lens and the Vermelles–Hulluch road

5.50am	Chlorine gas release from cylinders; gas moves slowly towards the German lines in the south (47th Division front), but lingers to the north, in the 15th and 1st Divisional fronts. Gas taps are turned off on the Grenay Spur, the location of the 1st Divisional front, following British gas casualties
6.20am	Gas taps turned on again; more British gas casualties in the 1st Division
6.30am	Zero hour, men of the 1/18th Battalion, the London Regiment kick a football towards the German lines; farther north, the Scots of the King's Own Scottish Borderers are piped out of their trenches by Piper Laidlaw, who would later that day receive the Victoria Cross for his actions. On the 1st Division front, attack is held up in front of Hulluch
7.30am	Men of the 47th Division in position at the right of the line, securing the Double Crassier
8am	Men of the 15th and 47th divisions largely clear the streets of Loos of German troops
9am	Germans regain Bois Carré on the 1st Division front
9.15am	Men of the 15th Division reach the Lens road
9.30am	Hill 70 captured; inadvertent change in direction of the attacking troops towards Lens and Cité St Laurent
10am	Loos village fully in British hands
10.55am	Composite 'Green's Force' attempts to carry the German lines to the north of the sector by frontal assault; it would be held

The Battlefield: What Actually Happened?

11.30am	German reinforcements at Cité St Laurent push back the advanced British troops
1pm	German counter-attack carries Hill 70
1.15pm	Major General Holland commits his 1st Division to an assault on Hulluch; assault continues for the rest of the day with little result. Hulluch would not fall

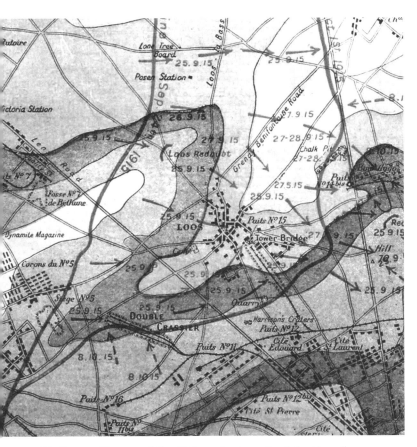

30. Topographic map of the IV Corps front, south of the Vermelles–Hulluch road, showing the village of Loos.

The corps boundary of the Vermelles–Hulluch road would prove to be of the greatest significance in the coming battle. For the IV Corps, south of the road, there would be the greatest initial success; but with the expectation that there would be sufficient reserves to back them up, there was to be nothing left in reserve in the corps itself. The attack would be all or nothing.

The London Territorials of the 47th Division were located in the southern part of the sector adjoining the French, south of the miners' villages at Grenay known as North and South Maroc, on the outskirts of Lens. It was naturally down to them that the distinctive pit-head gear of the Loos pylons had been nicknamed 'Tower Bridge'. At this point in the line the topography was more variable, with Grenay and Maroc occupying a spur and the mining village of Loos nestling in a shallow valley, the slopes of Hill 70 beyond. Fortunately, the men of the 47th Division had been trained in the assault on topography similar to this close to Noeux-les-Mines. The Londoners were given the task of capturing the frontline trenches in front of Loos to create a defensive position to the right of the line linking the spoil heaps of the Double Crassier (a double bank of spoil that extended some 1,200yds) to the Loos Crassier (a slagheap that intruded deeply into the village). In order to anchor the whole British advance, these London Territorial battalions were required to hold the line at all costs, preventing the Germans from outflanking the main line of the attack.

The gas cloud was released at 5.50am; given that the gas itself was heavier than air, despite the insignificant breeze, the chlorine was to hug the contours as planned and flow as a yellowish-green cloud downslope towards the village. At 6.30am, covered by a thick smoke barrage supplied by Stokes mortars, men of the division were to rise from their trenches or emerge from shallow Russian saps and advance down the slope in full view of the German trenches; it was essential that the gas and preliminary bombardment do their job. To confuse the Germans, dummies had been placed in no-man's-land in order to draw fire. At first, it

31. Men of the 47th Division advance forward on the morning of 25 September.

seemed that the German defenders were going to put up a stiff fight: there was wild machine-gun and rifle fire from the firesteps of the enemy trenches. This would soon change in the face of determined attacks by the Territorials between the two crassiers and the Loos–Bethune road.

The men of the London Irish Rifles (1/18th Battalion, London Regiment), on the left of the 47th Division line, north of the Double Crassier, would be first out of the trenches. The battalion was famous for footballing prowess, its team roundly beating others of the brigade, so it was perhaps not surprising that their entry into the 'big push' would involve kicking leather footballs forwards towards the German trenches. Officially frowned upon, one man, Private Edwards, would nevertheless carry a deflated ball into the line; inflating it before zero hour, he would launch

32. Soldier of the London Irish, the 1/18 Battalion, London Regiment, in 1915.

33. The Loos football, kicked off at zero hour, 25 September 1915.

the ball with a goalkeeper's throw, punting it towards the line while his colleagues followed it up:

> A boy came along the trench carrying a football under his arm. 'What are you going to do with that?' I asked. 'It's some idea this,' he said with a laugh. 'We're going to kick it across into the German trench.' 'It is some idea,' I said. 'What are our chances of victory in the game?'
>
> Patrick MacGill, *The Great Push*, 1915

The London Irish would soon drive the Germans from the line, pushing them back, causing them to stream through Loos and

THE MAN OF LOOS

The Man of Loos is a bronze statue on the war memorial of the London Irish Rifles, depicting a soldier in 1915 garb, holding a football. More remarkable is the preservation of the ball itself. Last seen by writer Patrick MacGill as a deflated leather bag on the German wire, it survived to become a celebrated relic of the Rifles' involvement in the battle. The exploit was repeated by the East Surrey Regiment at the opening of the Battle of the Somme.

back towards their second line. The football had reached its objective; hanging on the German wire, it would eventually find its way back to 'Blighty'.

With the London Irish in the enemy trenches, two other London battalions, south Londoners from Blackheath and Woolwich (1/20th Battalion), and north Londoners from St Pancras (1/19th Battalion), would push past the London Irish and assault the chalk pit on the Lens–La Bassée road (a strong position), as well as the mine workings of *Puits 15* – 'Tower Bridge' itself. To the right of the line, the men of the 1/6th and 1/7th London Regiment had secured their position on the Double Crassier by 7.30am; the line was safe from German outflanking movements from Lens.

In front of the chalk pit west of the Lens–La Bassée road, close to Hill 70, the enemy wire was largely uncut – and the fight would be intense, with hand grenades an important weapon, employed before the objective could be fully secured by 9.30am. For the St Pancras men, the attack on *Puits 15* would be fraught with difficulty, a machine-gun enfilading the line leading to the loss of many of the officers, including the colonel. This would be repeated at other parts of the line, the loss of senior officers disproportionate in this battle. Though the attack would stall,

34. Attack of the Scots of the 15th Division, 'Tower Bridge' in the background.

the disorganised 1/19th Battalion would nevertheless drive through the village, and would be reinforced by men of the reserve battalion, the Poplar and Stepney Rifles (1/17th London Regiment). By 10am, the village of Loos and its German defences were firmly in British hands.

North of the 47th Division, facing the north-western part of the village of Loos, lay the Scotsmen of the 15th Division. They were to assault the village south-eastwards, parallel to the Bethune–Lens and Vermelles–Loos roads, taking the German Loos defences before rising up from the Loos valley to the low slopes of Hill 70 behind – so named for its spot height of 70m above sea level.

PIPER LAIDLAW VC

Piper Laidlaw was a 40-year-old piper with the 7th KOSB. The role of the piper traditionally being to inspire the troops, Laidlaw was to take this seriously – seriously enough to earn him a Victoria Cross. With his company suffering from the release of gas, and in the face of the enemy bombardment, Piper Laidlaw leaped up on the parapet and, cutting an imposing figure, marched up and down, playing his company out of the trench. Later badly wounded by shellfire, Laidlaw continued in his duty, playing the pipes to inspire his comrades.

35. Piper Laidlaw VC.

The defences were well organised, with machine-gun equipped redoubts, and the Scots would have to face two such constructions built aside the roads and intended to stall any such advance: the Lens Road Redoubt (now the approximate site of Dud Corner CWGC cemetery) and the Loos Road Redoubt. Behind it, the German second line was also strong and so situated that, if the hill was to fall, it would be subjected to fire on three sides.

At zero hour, 6.30am, the Scotsmen rose from the trenches, the 9th Black Watch, 8th Seaforths, 10th Scottish Rifles, 7th King's Own Scottish Borderers (KOSB) and 12th Highland Light Infantry leading, and successive lines following in good order, emerging from the smoke and gas and making use of Russian saps that had been dug forwards. Though the ground sloped towards the village, the contours contrived to plateau here and there, and perhaps, as a consequence, the gas cloud lingered to the detriment of the leading British troops. For some men the exertions of the advance were countered by the heavy, dank, chemical-impregnated flannelette of the 'P' Helmet and they began to suffocate. Lifting the hood or rolling it up on the top of the head led to many men being affected by the lingering gas. It was here that Piper Laidlaw of the 7th KOSB would earn his Victoria Cross for piping the men forwards – continuing to do so in the advance, even though wounded.

This act of bravery by a lone piper would be much celebrated, and necessary, given the losses to officers suffered by the men of this K1 division. Pressing on, the assaulting battalions reached the Loos defences, only to be held up by the strength of the German wire, as yet uncut. Surging ahead, and reinforced by men of the 7th Camerons, the highlanders fought with cricket-ball grenades and bayonets, facing many defenders holed up in cellars and in the ruined streets of the contested village:

> We moved on towards the village of Loos, where machine guns were raking the streets and bayonet fighting was going on in full swing … most of the houses were blown in, but their

cellars were strongly built, and it was in these cellars that the Germans were mostly hiding.

CSM Thomas McCall, Cameron Highlanders

Joining with the St Pancras men of the 1/19th, the highlanders were finally successful in clearing the streets of Germans, with the village largely in British hands by 8am. Today, their assault is remembered by the location of the Loos British Cemetery, the majority of headstones marking unknown soldiers. To the north of the village, the German front was collapsing and the way was open for the soldiers to take Hill 70, one of the key defensive positions in the German second line. As the official historian, Sir James Edmonds, was to put it:

The Pylon Towers ['Tower Bridge'], well known to all ranks, now lay behind, and the men were in unfamiliar surroundings. The smoke that had made the atmosphere of Loos resemble a London fog had cleared, but their vision was bounded by the bare slope of Hill 70 in front of them, with its long bleak crest line some five hundred yards away outlined by the dull sky. There was no definite landmark against which to move … and the mass of men, now in considerable disorder advanced straight up the slope.

Brigadier General Sir James Edmonds

Famously resembling 'a bank holiday crowd', the exhilarated captors of Loos, some 1,500 of them, faced the hill. However, all was not well. With so many officer casualties, battalion cohesion started to break down, and though the 1/19th Londoners were intended to form a defensive screen to the south of the village, they mingled with the Scots of the 9th Black Watch. This created a tendency to stall and while the Germans streamed over the hill towards Lens their attackers followed, shifting southwards, opening up the attacking front and leaving their left flank –

which should have connected with the men of the 1st Division farther north – dangerously exposed. With the 1st Division held up, it was necessary to form a defensive flank, and the men of the 6th Cameron Highlanders were sent north of *Puits 14 bis* in order to protect the flank of the advanced British line, and to ensure that Hill 70 was similarly defended:

> Through a misunderstanding, about 500 of us went straight ahead towards Lens and passed a German redoubt where they were all holding their hands up in surrender … making our way through the gaps in the German barbed wire, we got into the outskirts of Lens, but were held up by machine gun and rifle fire and had to lie down and take cover.
>
> CSM Thomas McCall, 7th Cameron Highlanders

36. Attack of the 1st Division at Loos, as envisaged by a contemporary artist. The 'P' gas hoods were dank, clammy and suffocating.

Moreover, with an increasing number of Germans streaming southwards to the Lens suburb of Cité St Laurent, outside of the main battle area, a new threat appeared. From here, it would be possible for the Germans to mount a counter-attack and outflank the precariously held British line. The British would have to maintain their hold on the crest of Hill 70 – even though orders were issued that they should press forward to the mining village of Cité St Auguste, due east of the hill. Even with additional strengthening from the divisional reserves, and with supplies streaming into Loos, at around 1pm, the Germans were able to mount a counter-attack on the hill from the south and to carry it. The slippage of the attacking forces southwards around the flanks of the hill had cost them dearly and at nightfall the British line was stuck between the two German lines, their position precarious.

The final division of the IV Corps in the frontline was the 1st Division, a formation that had been in France from August 1914, and which was originally composed of regular battalions, now sorely depleted. Originally destined to be held in reserve, the division had been placed in the line north of the Vermelles–Hulluch road in early September. Here the regular battalions faced German lines on the low north-eastern extension of the Grenay spur, to the south of Hulluch. At this point the men of neither side could satisfactorily observe each other, as the German lines were just below the crest; and in an attempt to do so the Germans had dug two incomplete long saps ('northern' and 'southern') out towards the British lines. These were taken as the junction of the 15th and 1st divisions, but were not to be assaulted directly, leaving a gap in the line. There was also one distinctive feature of no-man's-land, the Lone Tree – a bare wreck of a cherry tree which was almost at the centre of the attacking front, 600yds north of the northern sap. Farther north was the small copse of Bois Carré (now the site of a CWGC cemetery). Attacking across the spur, the force would diverge, fanning out, and the centre would be filled by a force ('Green's Force') made from two Territorial battalions, the London Scottish (1/14th London Regiment) and the 1/9th King's Regiment, under the command of Lieutenant Colonel Green of the 2nd Royal Sussex.

When the gas was released in this sector, the unfavourable topography meant that it languished in the almost still air; without the benefit of the downhill slope, the gas started to move back towards the British trenches, helped by fluctuations in whatever wind was apparent. Here, famously, the men of the 2nd King's Royal Rifle Corps (KRRC) and the 1st Loyal North Lancs were to suffer casualties from their own gas, along with some of the men of the Royal Engineers Special Companies who released it. The gas was turned off. When the taps were opened once more at 6.20am, the wind again shifted in position, and the assaulting battalions were to suffer their own weapon turned against them. These brave men would have more than just gas and smoke fumes to contend with; the difficult topographical position meant that the bombardment was unable to find their target. This left the thick German wire uncut, the enemy machine-guns located at the Lone Tree and the northern sap untouched, the deep dugouts occupied. These factors would prove costly: the advance would be held up, stalled against the untouched German positions. It would have severe consequences for the 15th Division to the south, its flanks left hanging in the air.

North of the Lone Tree, two K3 battalions – the 10th Gloucesters and the 8th Royal Berkshires – were able to overrun the German trenches at great cost, and to surge through Bois Carré. They were followed up by the regular 1st Cameron Highlanders (whose fallen soldiers lie in nearby Ninth Avenue Cemetery, named after a German trench), who reached the outskirts of the village of Hulluch. Here a mixed force of the three battalions paused and the village was not assaulted. It would not be taken in this battle. Over the morning the German fire intensified over no-man's-land and the waiting men suffered intensely; by 9am the enemy had regained Bois Carré, establishing a strong position that would stand in the way of the British attempts to sweep them from the field. It would be down to Green's Force to take the line in a frontal assault. The force would not attack until 10.55am; vainly attempting to find a way through the thick barbed wire, the Liverpool men and the London Scots would be held up by the still-operating German machine-guns and would attempt to dig in with the help of their field-entrenching tools. Green's Force was held.

With no hope of taking the trenches in a frontal assault, Major General Holland, commanding the 1st Division, then committed his troops to an outflanking movement. The 2nd Welsh and the 2nd Munsters were able to gain a foothold, crossing no-man's-land to the north of Bois Carré (through another copse stranded in no-man's-land at La Haie), thereby managing by stealth to take the German first-line trench in reverse, and to halt on the main Lens–La Bassée road in front of Hulluch. The Germans of the 157th Regiment had no choice but to surrender, though to the south other members of this regiment attempted a counter-attack, but in vain. With the Welsh and Irish soldiers behind them, the combined Scots and English of Green's Force were able to push on to the German frontline. The German survivors gathered in Hulluch; but the depleted battalions of the British 1st Division were in no fit state to attempt to take the village, and made contact with the men of the 15th Division in their defensive flank. Hulluch would remain untaken, and would continue to be a thorn in the side of the British.

25 September 1915: I Corps

Attack on the frontage between the Vermelles–Hulluch road and La Bassée canal

5.50am	Gas released; gas moves towards the German lines on the 7th Divisional front; on the low-lying 2nd Division front, close to La Bassée canal, the gas stalls and causes numerous British gas casualties	

6.20am	British mine explodes south of La Bassée canal on the 2nd Division front; the crater was occupied by Germans; two more mines sprung farther south at 6.28am, again with no appreciable result
6.30am	Zero hour; men of the 7th Division advance through no-man's-land to carry the German first line; north of the Auchy–Vermelles road it would stall, with British gas casualties; here the main German Madagascar Trench would be held. On the 2nd Divisional front, the German wire was largely uncut and the negative effects of the gas release stall the British attack
7.10am	Men of the 9th Division carry the Hohenzollern Redoubt; by 7.30am they had captured *Fosse 8* behind it
8.45am	The 2nd Gordons reach the Lens road and Pekin Trench; this would be the advance position of the 9th Division
9.30am	The quarries in front of St Elie are captured and consolidated by men of the 7th Division. The attack on the 7th Division front would stall here. By midnight the Germans would retake this position
9.45am	Attack of the 2nd Division stalls in their original positions
12.15pm	Further assault on Madagascar Trench by the 7th Division fails
5pm	Pekin Trench, on the 7th Division front, is abandoned to the Germans

North of the Vermelles–Hulluch road, responsibility passed from the IV Corps to the I Corps, commanded by Lieutenant General Hubert Gough. In this sector, the influence of the rolling spur terrain descending from the Artois plateau was much reduced. Here was the flat, open plain described by Haig in the damning report submitted to Sir John French earlier in the summer. Haig's expectation was that

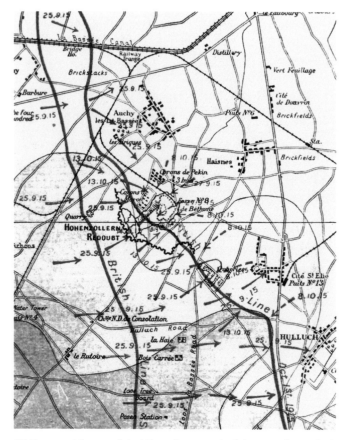

37. Topographic map of the I Corps front, north of the Vermelles–Hulluch road, showing the flat terrain.

this would be a particularly shell-blasted and machine-gun swept piece of ground; a view that was not to be challenged by events. The main German observation position was *Fosse 8*, easily picked out by its tall slagheap, situated in the vicinity of the Cité de Madagascar. South-west of Auchy-les-Mines, Madagascar was a small village, like many others in the region, that had been encapsulated into the German lines and was heavily fortified.

The British plan here was simple: three divisions would assault the German advanced line after the preliminary bombardment and then, with the release of gas and smoke, press on through to the German second-line trench and beyond. Though Haig had originally been more than sceptical about the chances of British success here, he was buoyed by the possibilities provided by the use of gas, and therefore expected a breakthrough, the assaults north and south of the bisecting Vermelles–Hulluch road punching through the strong German second line, which was arraigned along the north–south oriented Lens–La Bassée route. Standing in the way of the I Corps, however, were strong fortifications, the most famous of which were the works known as the Hohenzollern Redoubt.

Adjoining the IV Corps, and the 1st Division, was another nominally 'regular' formation, the 7th Division, which had already seen much action in Flanders since arriving in Belgium almost a year before. To this formation was allotted the task of taking the line immediately to the west of Hulluch and, farther to the north, the village of Cité St Elie. Here, as with almost the whole of its length, the German lines were fortified with strongpoints, including one christened the 'Pope's Nose' that jutted out towards the British lines and provided opportunity for enfilading fire against any attackers. It would fulfil its promise. As with the situation close to Hill 70 farther south, there were also a small number of chalk pits that provided good opportunity for defence. Long grass covering the slopes made observation difficult.

Here conditions were variable for the dispersion of the gas, but in the main it was effective. They were too effective in some situations, and the unpleasant dank suffocating 'P' Helmets were once again to play their part in tempting the British soldiers to remove them and risk being gassed themselves. Nevertheless, the combined efforts of the gas release and the artillery bombardment – which here had been effective in breaching the wire – meant that close to the Vermelles–Hulluch road (a

38. The quarries at Hulluch, still in German hands prior to the battle.

route which was also to be later exploited by a battery of RHA, the guns brought up at a gallop) the 2nd Gordon Highlanders and the 8th Devonshires were able to reach the German frontline position, here named Breslau Trench. Circumstances were difficult, though, and here, as with other parts of the line, numerous officer casualties were suffered in the process, most of them just in front of the enemy wire. Both battalions were to push on to the Lens road behind, crossing the German communication trenches in front of Hulluch, in an attempt to reach the second line and *Stutzpunkt II*. The work of the artillery in damaging the wire in the frontline was not replicated in front of the second line; here the Gordons halted.

Farther north, the quarries were to provide an obstacle to the assault that would hold up the 1st South Staffordshires and 2nd Royal Warwickshires. The initial assault was also held up by the thick wire, again uncut, though this would be overcome by the force of the advance; and together with the reserve battalion of the 2nd Queen's, the quarries would fall and be organised for defence by the British. The assault, stalled in front of St Elie, would not be resumed.

North of the regular 7th Division was another of Kitchener's armies, the 9th, a Scottish division, composed of battalions of Kitchener's army made famous by Ian Hay's book, *The First Hundred Thousand* (1915). The 9th had much in common with the 15th Division that had attacked as part of the IV Corps, though while the 15th Division had as its target the northern defences of Loos, the 9th Division faced another formidable position: the Hohenzollern Redoubt, with 300yds of heavily wired trenches. Ian Hay would describe it in his book:

> The Hohenzollern Redoubt … is a most inconspicuous object, but a very important factor in the present situation. It has been thrust forward from the Bosche lines to within a hundred yards of our own – a great promontory, a maze of trenches, machine gun emplacements, and barbed wire, all flush with or under the ground, and terribly difficult to cripple with shell fire.
>
> Ian Hay, *The First Hundred Thousand*, 1915

39. Uncut wire of the Loos defences.

Behind the redoubt was flattened slagheap of *Fosse 8*:

> Fosse 8 is a mighty waste-heap such as you may behold
> anywhere along the railway in the colliery districts between
> Glasgow and Edinburgh. The official map calls such an
> eminence a Fosse; the Royal Engineers call it a Dump;
> Operation Orders call it a Slag-Heap; experts [in the Division]
> call it a bing.

Ian Hay, The First Hundred Thousand, 1915

It is hardly surprising that Hay would refer to Loos as the 'Battle
of the Slagheaps'. Cut through *Fosse 8* with a network of tunnels
and interconnected trenches, the two works were a formidable
obstacle to progress. It was fortunate, however, that there were
two British 9.2in howitzers trained upon the redoubt – and that
their fire was accurate, destroying wire and helping stove in at
least part of the works.

The assault on the redoubt was led by the 7th Seaforths and the
5th Cameron Highlanders, distinguished amongst other things by
the style of their Glengarries, plain for the Camerons and diced for
the Seaforths. Russian saps assisted the progress of the battalion,
which had to emerge through a cloud of gas and smoke that
lingered close to the British lines, yet forming a protective screen
for the advancing line to develop. The assault would be short and
sharp, and with the artillery having achieved its aim, the attacking
Scots found themselves in control of a communication trench,
Corons Trench, that ran to the rear of *Fosse 8*. This trench and
its extension would mark the final point of the advance, as the
leading battalions halted to consolidate their positions, though
not without the Germans attempting to flood the trench – an
unwelcome feature that would require the ministrations of the
divisional engineers.

With these strongpoints grasped, there was an immediate
need to try to assault the strong second line behind and therefore

40. View of the defensive position of the Hohenzollern Redoubt on the day of the attack, picked out by the lines of chalk.

to effect a breakthrough. Here the line was known as Pekin Trench, which, though shallow, was protected by a belt of wire entanglements that stretched some 15yds across. Despite the ministrations of the British artillery to the fortifications developed in the frontline, there was no opportunity to take on the strong line here. It would be the 12th Royal Scots who would get through the wire to take the trench, joined by the 11th Royal Scots and the 8th Gordons, who would have to try to defend the line fiercely, their flanks in their air.

Grimly, the Scots held on in the face of bombing attacks by the Germans, whose long 'potato masher' grenades carried much farther than the heavy, spherical cricket-ball grenades carried by the Scots, bombs that required ignition through the act of

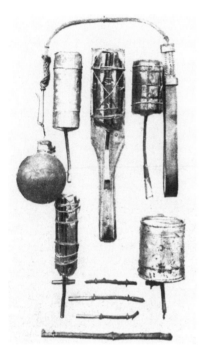

41. Grenades. British extemporised grenades (left) and the effective German 'potato masher' (right).

striking on a cardboard friction lighter. Like any box of matches, however, such strikers soon became useless in damp conditions. Under pressure, the reserve battalion, the 6th Royal Scots Fusiliers, were sent forward but, stuck in the mud and caught up in the confusion, they would take four hours to struggle forwards and their numbers soon dwindled under constant German attacks. Pekin Trench would be retaken, the British survivors retiring to Fosse Alley, which would mark the furthest advance in this sector, the relieving 10th Argyll and Sutherland Highlanders already having halted here. Held in the face of concerted German attacks, the men would nevertheless wend their way back from this advanced position to the German frontline, worn out and weary.

North of the Vermelles–Auchy road, the frontline from the Hohenzollern Redoubt continued into a line of front known as Madagascar Trench, so named for the small group of mine dwellings developed on the road to Auchy. Here the Germans had created defences that had much in common with the early history of siege warfare: pits filled with stakes and covered with turf. More conventional barbed wire entanglements were also a major issue, especially as they remained uncut. Also, jutting from the line close to the Vermelles road were machine-gun-equipped strongpoints that were to enfilade the leading units attacking the trench. Here the 6th King's Own Scottish Borderers would be fatally held up, the gas and smoke discharge having been ineffectual. Losing all their officers, the few Scots survivors were forced to crawl back to their start point under fire. The attack of the 10th Highland Light Infantry would have a similar outcome, this time caught in the open by machine-guns sited in another strongpoint along the line, Railway Redoubt. These guns, and the effects of the lingering gas cloud here (a function of weak and changeable breezes), would account for 85 per cent of the casualties within the battalion within just 20yds of their start positions. The ineffectual nature of the opening bombardment, coupled with the poverty of the gas cloud, had left the 10th Highland Light Infantry with a hopeless frontal assault. Though a second assault was ordered by the corps commander at mid-morning, it would be to little avail. Here the attack was stalled, no ground gained. To the south, the men in the Hohenzollern Redoubt were in a precarious position.

The remaining division of I Corps was the 2nd, a regular formation that had fought at Mons in August 1914, and that was now to attack along a broad stretch of front that would cross La Bassée canal before adjoining the Indian Corps north of Givenchy. Attacking over the low ground either side of the canal, the 2nd Division would also have to assault the brickfields at Cuinchy, stacks of bricks compiled during the peacetime operations

42. *British grenade attack in the I Corps sector.*

of the area. These stacks added to the topographical confusion that faced the British troops, and had been built into the German lines, equipped with machine-gun nests. The area was also complicated by the results of a considerable amount of mine warfare that had been fought in a largely unco-ordinated manner in the months before the battle. Craters pockmarked the ground here and were to prove difficult to cross. Further mines would be blown close to zero hour, but, in a classic mistake, there was a ten-minute delay. This would allow the German defenders the opportunity to occupy the rim of the crater before the British could advance and would represent a lost opportunity, particularly as the Germans manned the craters with machine-guns that would wreak havoc with the British lines. Other mines would also be blown and would also be ineffectual, the opportunity wasted when they blew up portions of the German frontline that were unoccupied.

Nevertheless, intended to support the 'big push' farther to the south, the 2nd Division was given just limited objectives, gaining control of a German communication trench such that it created a defensive flank that would mirror the one that was supposed to have been formed between the two crassiers at the southern margin of the attack. The attack did not open in auspicious circumstances. On release, the gas and smoke was actively carried back towards the attackers, who had to rely on their stuffy and suffocating smoke helmets. Here, in this low-lying place, it was not possible to rely on topography to drive the gas forwards and a breeze offered resistance to their aims, blowing the gas backwards. In places the gas officers refused to open the taps on the gas cylinders, quite properly, in the face of the conditions; they were nevertheless forced to release the gas:

> The gas men rushed about shouting and asking each other for the loan of an adjustable spanner. They discharged one or two cylinders with the spanners that they had; the gas went whistling out, formed a thick cloud a few yards away in No Man's Land, and then gradually spread back into the trenches.
>
> Lt Robert Graves, 2nd Royal Welsh Fusiliers

Pooling in the frontline, the gas badly affected the men of the 2nd South Staffordshires close to the canal – over a hundred would be marked as gas casualties. With the gas ineffectual, and no smoke to cover the attack, the Germans were able to bring rifle and machine-gun fire to bear. This situation would be repeated up and down the 2nd Division's frontage, and it was here that the gas was the least effective. This, battle confusion and the fact that the German barbed wire was once more thick and uncut meant that the attacks failed, the defenders using their superior hand grenades to good effect. Though the brave battalions of the 2nd Division pressed forward, their attack was spent – and, like efforts of the adjoining 9th Division, they would see out the end of the day in their original positions, but at great loss to them, in both officers and men.

At the close of 25 September, the anticipated breakthrough had not happened. The IV Corps came closest to their objectives in taking the village of Loos, but stalled at Hill 70. However, the leading battalions of the 47th and 15th divisions lost direction in their advance and, in their enthusiasm – and lacking officers – had swung southwards towards the strong positions on the outskirts of Lens. Movement along the Vermelles–Hulluch road allowed some penetration towards Hulluch itself, but here the advance once more stalled, momentum lost. The attack on the Hohenzollern Redoubt, supported by accurate and intense shellfire, meant that this position, perhaps the strongest in the line, was taken – but again opportunities were lost in pressing on to the German second line, the fog of war and fatigue playing its part alongside the inadequacy of the British grenades in the face of the superior German 'potato masher'.

Everywhere else, the attacks had stalled due to four all too apparent reasons. Firstly, with the atmospheric conditions poor, the gas release relied upon the fact that the chlorine was heavier than air and therefore required forward slopes to drive the gasses towards the enemy lines. As topography varied north of Loos, this was not always going to happen – with the result that gas could be driven into the face of the attackers, or be blown or flow backwards towards the British frontline. The clammy and

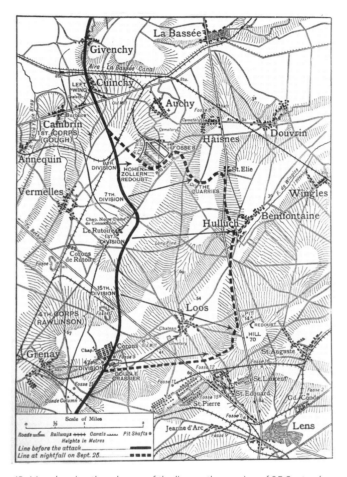

*43. Map showing the advance of the line on the evening of 25 September.
The deepest penetration had been in the IV Corps area.*

suffocating British respirators would also play their part, and
men would be gassed accordingly. Secondly, the British artillery,
long known to be limited in strength and supposed to be backed
up by the gas, achieved limited and variable effectiveness. In
places the wire was cut, defences destroyed, but for the most

part the artillery was ineffectual. Thirdly, casualties had been high amongst the British ranks, especially so amongst officers, whose losses were surely disproportionate. The great gallantry of the attackers was reduced in effect by the loss of their officers – many of them senior in rank. Lacking in leadership, the attacks lost direction. Finally, the spirited defence of the limited German forces was sufficient to sap the forward momentum of, in many cases, the inexperienced British divisions.

As night fell, the situation was becoming extremely precarious for the survivors of the forward battalions all along the line at Loos. For those in advanced positions, the inadequacy of the advance meant that their flanks were exposed, vulnerable to enemy counter-attacks. There had to be some important decisions made if the attack was to be resumed the next day. The British held on grimly.

Reinforcement would be necessary – and here General Haig would call upon his reserves, in the form of the XI Corps.

24–25 September: The Movement of XI Corps

Movement forward of the First Army reserves

	20–23 September	Landing of the 21st and 24th divisions in France, and movement to Lilliers in two night marches
24th	7pm	Night march of 21st and 24th divisions to advanced positions commences
	25 September	
	2am	Men of 21st and 24th Divisions start arriving in their positions
25 September	6am	Last men of 21st and 24th Divisions reach their advanced positions
	7.15am	3rd Cavalry Division in position at Vaudricourt, 5 miles west of Vermelles

25 September	**9.30am**	Field Marshal Sir John French releases the two divisions to General Haig's Command; Haig would only become aware of this two hours later
	10.30am	3rd Cavalry Division ordered forward to Vermelles
	11.30am	The two divisions make their final march forward to their advanced positions in preparation for the next day's attack
	12.40pm	Major General Briggs of the 3rd Cavalry Division advises General Haig that an assault by the division would not be feasible

It was planned that the corps reserves would comprise two novice Kitchener's army (K3) divisions, the 21st and 24th. Closest to the line was the 24th, formed along the line of La Bassée canal near Bethune, with the 21st at the boundary of the Franco–British forces, to the west of Noeux-les-Mines. Sir John French had earlier commented unfavourably on the creation of divisions of Kitchener's army men:

> The experience I have gained during the war leads me to a very decided conclusion that it would not be advisable to organise troops so raised and so trained … in any higher units than brigades … I feel quite sure that to put an Army, corps or even a division composed of these troops … straight into the field under commanders and staff who are inexperienced in up-to-date European warfare, might easily become a positive danger.
>
> Field Marshal Sir John French, January 1915

His view had changed volte-face by September, believing, according to Sir James Edmonds, that new divisions fresh from training might have been free from the 'trench habit' – in other words, that they might be more inclined to leave the trenches and funkholes, and push forwards. However, for the military theorist Sir Basil Liddell-Hart, writing in 1930, the decision to use these unseasoned men still appeared contrary:

With curious judgment French left seasoned divisions [with III Corps] lying idle on the quiet Somme front, and chose to use these two raw divisions for the critical phase of the battle. Moreover, he had given Haig to understand that they would be immediately at hand for Haig's use, whereas he placed them sixteen miles in the rear.

Basil Liddell-Hart, *A History of the World War, 1914–1918*

In addition to these K3 divisions there was the 3rd Cavalry Division – there to exploit any breakthrough, should there be one – and the Guards Division, assembled from the Guards battalions already in France in August 1915.

Haig had made his original battle plans for Loos on the basis that all its component divisions would be present to press on the attack. This view was understandably formed on the statement made by the British commander-in-chief to General Foch in August, that the attack would be made using six divisions, with two divisions in reserve; Haig took this to mean that, as commander of the First Army, he would have control of the whole. However, Sir John was to differ in his opinion. Whether undecided as to the best course of action or whether trying to maintain a modicum of control over the battle, French was committed to keeping hold of these troops. He would control the general reserves directly, and he would keep them close, in the vicinity of Lilliers, some 15 miles away from the frontline. Nevertheless, he was to issue orders that would give Haig some hope that there would be movement at the opening of the battle, and that these men would be transferred to his control. He was to be disappointed. Sir John would later claim that this reserve was made available to Haig as the variable achievements along the line became known. Haig would claim otherwise.

The battle of words between French and Haig commenced even as the offensive was in progress, and with the men of the I and IV Corps hammering away at the entrenched line of the

German *VI Armeekorps*. Reports from the battle front were of variable quality, but all seemed to imply that by force of arms the British troops were standing on the verge of a breakthrough and that at Hill 70, the Hohenzollern Redoubt, and along the Vermelles–Hulluch road there existed chances to press on and break the deadlock – so long as there were sufficient troops to move forward. Deployment of the XI Corps divisions was therefore essential to guarantee success. Separating the Guards Division off, Sir John belatedly agreed to move the 21st and 24th divisions closer to the front, expecting them to move to Noeux-les-Mines and Beury respectively, still miles away from the front.

In fact, the movement of the XI Corps had started much earlier, from the landing of the 21st and 24th divisions in France (and the formation of the Guards Division) in early September with a movement towards the concentration point at St Omer; from here the corps started its long train of movement on 20 September, the soldiers marching by night to avoid enemy observation. It would be a gruelling march forward, with over 20 miles covered in the first two nights, arriving at Lilliers on the 23rd. Though theoretically rested during the days following these night marches, most of the men were unaccustomed to sleeping in daylight and the adjustment was difficult. When the orders came through that they should move to their advanced positions for the morning of 25 September, the two K3 divisions were readied with orders that they should prepare to be self-sufficient on their route to the front, and that this self-sufficiency was to last until at least 27 September.

In addition to their normal accoutrements, these men would be expected to go into battle in full marching order; that is they should carry their greatcoats in packs and maintain additional food rations in their haversacks. The march to their advanced positions was intended to be straightforward, a matter of a few hours from their start time of 7pm on the 24th. However, this expectation had not factored in the crush of traffic coming and going from the battle front, and of the many minor irritations and inconveniences that would together militate against the efficient movement of these inexperienced troops. There would be poor traffic marshalling; narrow roads shared with motor and horse transport; stoppages at railway crossings; and, in one infamous case, the hold up of a brigade commander by a military policeman. Instead of the projected three hours, it would take six or seven hours. Both General Haig and the corps commander, Major General Haking, were damning in their condemnation of the two divisions, stating that the delay 'was caused chiefly by their own indifferent march discipline', a slur on the quality of the divisions that would have far-reaching significance. Nevertheless, the Guards were struggling forward too:

> The road was frequently blocked, and halts were numerous. We met many ambulances returning with the wounded, and once I had to halt my company to allow a party of English and Indian troops to pass who had succumbed to our own gas.
>
> Captain Roland Feilding, 3rd Coldstream Guards

In an often quoted analogy, the official historian would compare the movement of the divisions to 'trying to push the Lord Mayor's procession through the streets of London without clearing the route and holding up the traffic'. Clearly not optimal conditions.

The exhausted divisions started to reach their advanced positions – still 5 miles from the frontline – in the early hours of the morning of 25 September, most cases dead on their feet. The last men arrived at 6am; exhausted, all fell out to gather whatever respite they could in the damp atmosphere of the early morning, resting fitfully as their comrades in the I and IV Corps struggled against the German lines at zero hour, 6.30am. It was not until much later that Sir John French would release them to the control of General Haig – nominally at 9.30am (as published in Sir John's dispatch of 15 October 1915), but in actuality at least two hours later. Haig had been pushing French to release the troops, but he had been absent from his headquarters; it took a visit to Haig from the commander-in-chief to confirm the transference of command.

Haig had, in the meantime, ordered the 3rd Cavalry Division forward to exploit what he considered was a developing breakthrough in the German line. From 7.15am the division had been ready at Vaudricourt, 5 miles to the west of Vermelles; Haig wanted the division to be in a position of strength closer to the line. With his confidence that the use of gas would double the effectiveness of the artillery preparation and the feeling that there could be a decisive breakthrough, in common with the French generals, Haig had always planned to exploit any breaks within the line with his mobile troops. At 10.30am he ordered them to move to an advanced position close to Vermelles. From here the divisional commander, Major General Briggs, made an advanced reconnaissance of the developing situation close to the frontline. Far from seeing a gaping hole in the German defences, from the advanced headquarters of the 1st, 7th and 15th divisions, he was to learn of the struggles of the British to push forward at the left of the line. Briggs knew that there would not be an opportunity for his cavalry to charge the lines and rout the Germans. When General Haig ordered the advance at 12.40pm Briggs was to warn him that this was not possible. Nevertheless, Haig (characterised by Nick Lloyd as a serial optimist) was to order General Haking to move the majority of the 21st and 24th divisions forward into the sector between Loos and Hulluch. Haking, believing that both Hulluch and Hill 70 (the strongpoint behind Loos) had fallen, complied.

Four brigades of the two new army divisions would attempt an assault on the German second line arraigned along the Hulluch–Lens road. They were to move into battle position on yet another trying night march – but with one difference. Tired of experiencing congestion and confusion along the roads and tracks leading to the front, they would attempt a night march across country, more often than not depending on compass bearings, taken in darkness and using maps at a scale of 1:100,000, if they had maps at all. The long grass of the open landscape to the north of Loos was extremely confusing and wearisome, and in mist and dampness the two divisions struggled to get forward in the dark cloudy night, the only light available being that from the burning village of Loos, which had been bombarded heavily by the German artillery. Also, confronting them were the original trenches of the British and German frontlines, which presented as deep ditches to the tired and fully laden troops. As noted by the official historian:

> Without having been in action before or having seen a shot fired, these troops were actually confronted with a difficult situation on unknown ground, without guidance from commanders or staffs who had been in the sector and studied the features for months past.
>
> Brigadier General Sir James Edmonds

Exhausted, they gained their advanced positions in front of the German second line, ready for the assault later that morning. The attack was to take place at 11am.

26 September 1915: The Crucial Day

Resuming the attack, and deployment of the XI Corps

| 26 September | 9am | 15th Division, reinforced by the 62nd Brigade (21st Division), assaults Hill 70 following a preliminary bombardment of one hour. The attack would fail |
| | 9am | German counter-attack from Cité St Auguste to Bois Hugo repulsed, though at great loss |

	11am	1st Division attacks at Hulluch, while the remainder of the 21st and 24th divisions attack on a narrow front between Bois Hugo and Hulluch. The attack would falter
	12.20pm	The attacks stall, both divisions begin to fall back to their original start point; the line would later be stabilised by the arrival of the Guards Division

While General Haking's men moved into their positions, the Germans were not content to sit back and watch the offensive continue. They had been rattled, certainly; and in some cases they prepared to retreat in the face of what was considered to be an irreparable gap in their lines. However, as the fog cleared from the battlefield during the late morning of 25 September, the Germans were able to make a more reasonable assessment of the situation. The *Reichsheer* had held the British at several key points, and these strongpoints were arresting the movement of the I and IV corps.

Recognising the precarious nature of the situation of those British divisions that had managed to push forwards (particularly those who had managed to exploit the Vermelles–Hulluch road in driving on to the outskirts of Hulluch, and at Hill 70 in the more southerly part of the line), the Germans reinforced their lines and prepared for counter-attack. Some twenty-two additional battalions were moved into position in the line that night, and the German second line would become stronger than ever before; stronger, in fact, than their original first line had been in meeting the assault of the British at the opening of the day. Not prepared to sit back, the Germans also launched counter-attacks against the British, most notably against Hill 70 to the south of the line, and against the men of the 7th and 9th Divisions holding the quarries just to the north of the Vermelles–Hulluch road, in front of *Fosse 8*. The precarious line manned by the 15th Division on the western slopes of Hill 70, below its insubstantial summit, would be held, just. However, at

44. The quarries in front of Hulluch; in British hands, for now.

the quarries the Germans would be more successful; they would be in charge of this strongpoint as dawn broke.

While these fights were in progress, and with the undermanned XI Corps in progress towards their eventual start point, Sir Douglas Haig made his plans to resume the general offensive on the 26th, from Hill 70 through to Cité St Elie, just north of Hulluch, and just behind *Fosse 8*. Commencing at 11am, the 15th Division, reinforced by the 62nd Brigade of the 21st Division (men of the Northumberland Fusiliers, East Yorkshires and the Yorkshire Regiment who had been separated from the main mass of the XI Corps before its fateful night march), would attempt to force Hill 70 and anchor the British right flank here. To the north, the 1st Division (IV Corps) was to attack at Hulluch, south of the Vermelles road, while the I Corps would throw its weight against Cité St Elie north of the same road. To the remaining brigades of the 21st and 24th Divisions (XI Corps) would fall the responsibility of assaulting the German line between Bois Hugo, a small wood just behind *Puits 14 bis* on the Lens–La Bassée road, and the southern margin of Hulluch. This would be a narrow

45. 'Tower Bridge', Puits 14 bis (right) and Hill 70 (left).

front to deploy these men, already exhausted from their night-time exertions.

The attack on Hill 70 was doomed to failure. Failing to hold it on the first day had been a costly mistake. The attack commenced with a desultory artillery preparation, hampered by the advanced nature of the lines and the supply of artillery ammunition. Though some guns had moved forward, it was difficult to supply them. Listed for the attack were men of the 15th Division (45th Brigade: 13th Royal Scots, 7th Royal Scots Fusiliers and 11th Argyll & Sutherlands), to be followed up by a brigade of the 21st Division (62nd Brigade: 12th Northumberland Fusiliers and 10th Yorkshires). Like so many similar features across Flanders, Hill 70 was subdued, and yet its capture was essential:

> Hill 70 rose above us darkly. It scarcely deserves the name of hill; quite a moderate rise, but that night it appeared intensely black and forbidding against the flaring lights that gleamed intermittently in the sullen sky behind it.
>
> Pte W. Walker, Northumberland Fusiliers

46. Soldier from the 2nd Welsh Regiment, 1st Division.

With the men hopelessly mixed in the assault trenches, and with poor maps misleading the newcomers, the attack soon ran out of steam, driven back by the weight of artillery and machine-gun fire. As the German fire intensified, the attempt broke, the men streaming back to Loos. Hill 70 would remain untaken:

> The shellfire was deafening enough, but the clatter that commenced with our further advance was abominable. It was as if the enemy were attacking with a fleet of motorcycles – it was the hellish machine guns. Our chaps fell like grass under the mower, mostly shot in the guts; so well had he got our range.
>
> Pte W. Walker, Northumberland Fusiliers

The attempt to take Hulluch was in the hands of the IV Corps, and specifically the 1st Division, men who had already suffered much in the preceding day's assaults; the attack would be made by three sub-strength battalions: the 2nd Welsh, 1st Black Watch and 1st South Wales Borderers. The attack itself was delayed by reports of German movements forward; but when the Welsh finally got up to the Lens–La Bassée road, these Germans retired, and the Welshmen found themselves in advance of the right of the line. The attack was stalled; but by the time it was resumed at midday, the Germans had composed themselves enough to pour fire into the ragged British formations. Their attack was called off and Hulluch once more remained untaken.

By midday on 26 September, the flanks of the proposed British advance on the centre of the battle front, between the fortified villages of Hulluch and Cité St Auguste just behind the Lens–La Bassée road, were unsecured. Assigned to this sector were the remainder of the untried, tired and hungry battalions of the 21st and 24th divisions. This was the very ground that was considered most unfavourable by Haig to French in his report of August 1915. In the plans for the opening day of the Battle of Loos, Haig had factored in four days of artillery bombardment, its effects magnified by the use of poison gas, a force multiplier that he hoped would double the effect of the artillery. With the resources spent and the hard-fought battles of the previous day inconclusive, Haig and his three corps commanders were faced with difficult choices. Though some of the artillery had been moved forward, there still remained the insurmountable problem of ammunition supply. This had limited the preliminary bombardments of the strongpoints of Hill 70 and Hulluch to just one hour (the batteries of the two divisions moving forward under the cover of darkness) and there would be no gas to support it. There was a need to tackle the open ground of the central sector (past the battlefield feature that became known as the Lone Tree) defended by a strong German second line containing at least three strongpoints (*Stützpunkt III*, *IV* and *V*), part of what the official historian would refer to as 'the curtain of a great bastioned front'. To assault these defences, getting stronger by the minute, artillery would be sorely needed. As before, the bombardment would be limited to just a single hour. The men were in poor condition, suffering from their exertions. As noted by the official historian:

> The men, wet through, had passed a sleepless and trying night, and this after a series of night marches. In spite of tremendous efforts, it had been impossible to bring the ration wagons and cookers up. The leaders were in an even more unhappy state of mind, for there was a complete absence of information as to the general situation and the exact position of the various battalions.
> Brigadier General Sir James Edmonds

As if to compound the difficulties, before the allotted British zero hour of 11am, the Germans had counter-attacked from Cité St Auguste (the site of the present-day Aérodrome de Lens-Benifontaine, north of the A21 autoroute) through to Bois Hugo, on the southern flank of Hill 70. Penetrating into the lines of the leading brigade of the 21st Division at around 9am, the men of the 8th Lincolnshires, enfiladed, were forced back. The German attacks had to be countered by the 8th Somerset Light Infantry and the 10th York and Lancashires before the main assault could begin. The battle that ensued would be fierce and would see the loss of the senior officers of the 63rd Brigade, including its commander, Brigadier General Nickalls. At the point of collapse of the British line, the 14th Durham Light Infantry (DLI) advanced. Losing most of its officers, the Durham men would suffer badly before being followed up by its sister battalion, the 15th DLI, attacking at the time of the general advance, at 11am.

To the north, the 24th Division – just six battalions of its total – was facing the Lone Tree positions, adjoining the 9th Division (I Corps) holding the line in front of *Fosse 8*. In the early hours of the morning, the absence of definite orders meant that a staff officer, Major Sir W. Kay, had to be sent to divisional headquarters near Vermelles to gain any idea of what was meant to happen on their front. Returning at 9.45am, he was to explain to the brigade commanders that the 72nd Brigade (8th Queen's, 9th East Surrey, 8th Buffs and 8th Royal West Kent) was to attack the German second line between *Stutzpunkt IV* and *Stutzpunkt III*, the others remaining in reserve. With ten minutes to spare, the attack was organised and the assault went ahead, under the most trying circumstances, at 11am. With the losses to the 21st Division farther south, the weight of arms thrown against the strong German positions had dwindled alarmingly.

The attack of the four brigades of the combined 21st and 24th divisions would ultimately result in what the Germans came to know, dramatically, as the *Leichenfeld von Loos* (the field of corpses), a corpse-strewn field in front of the still intact and strengthened German line north of Loos on 26 September. It would be described by Roland Feilding of the Guards Division, which had been brought up to strengthen the attack and intended to take their position at the low spur of land at Lone Tree. Feilding was to experience the after effects of the battle first hand:

47. View back over the desolate battlefield, from the maximum advance of the British in front of Hulluch; destined to be the Leichenfeld von Loos.

Hopwood and I crossed our old frontline and Noman's [sic] land – here about 500 yards wide – past the Lone Tree to the German trenches. The ground was strewn with our dead, and in all directions were wounded men crawling on their hands and knees. It was piteous …

Captain Roland Feilding, 3rd Coldstream Guards

With the residue of the 21st and 24th Divisions attacking over the difficult ground, the Germans took every advantage to organise for defence. The most difficult conditions were experienced to the right of the British advance, the German possession of Bois Hugo in advance of their second-line position, providing ample opportunity for enfilading machine-gun fire. The 6th Cameron Highlanders expended themselves trying to dislodge them from the wood – to no avail, and with heavy losses. Hill 70 still loomed large on the right flank, and the attacking battalions of the 21st Division started to wheel around to the south-east, British soldiers on the slopes of the hill being mistaken for Germans in their long greatcoats and gas helmets. This brought the men of the 64th Brigade (9th and 10th King's Own Yorkshire Light Infantry (KOYLI)) into danger, the German machine-guns from Bois Hugo and nearby Chalet wood opening fire. By 12.20pm the attack here had faltered, the Yorkshiremen retiring back to the Loos–Hulluch road. The attempt to break the line had broken down itself.

Farther to the north, the 24th Division was at least able to approach the German second line. Attacking at zero hour, the 72nd Brigade moved forwards, supported by two battalions of the 71st. These men were to suffer the full weight of the German artillery and machine-gun fire from both Hulluch, still firmly in German hands, and Bois Hugo to the south. The narrowness of the attacking front was once more telling on the attackers. The advancing British troops could observe the thickness of the uncut German wire ahead of them protecting the German second line, and they were bombarded with shells, including those filled with gas. The Germans were visibly standing up in the trenches in order to get a better sight of their targets. It would not be long before the tenacity of the attacking troops was worn out, and by late morning their bolt had been pretty much shot. The British attackers wavered in their assault and began to fall back; they were not to stop until they reached the original British frontline, some 4,000yds in the rear. The two divisions were broken; General Haking, the XI Corps commander in his headquarters in Nouex-les-Mines, would at first dismiss reports of their defeat as exaggerated and alarmist. General Haig would order the Guards Division forwards to take their place in the line.

The attack and retirement of the untried divisions would also result in post-battle acrimony between the commanders and general condemnation of the quality of the troops and their training, which would downplay the almost continuous march forwards of these K3 divisions over successive nights in the most trying of conditions. After another difficult march to the front, the Guards took up their positions, stretching from the eastern margins of Loos and arcing back towards the original German first line and the Lone Tree. Hill 70 was firmly in German hands, as was Bois Hugo – which had done so much damage. Behind the steady line created by the Guards Division, the men of the 21st and 24th divisions formed up. Their casualties had been heavy.

Though overplayed by Alan Clark in his book *The Donkeys* – who claimed that the two divisions lost over 8,000 men with no losses to the Germans in little over an hour – the two divisions would suffer badly when committed. As Sir Basil Liddell-Hart put it, writing in 1930:

> Tired, hungry, and as confused as their commanders, they were launched to the attack … without effective artillery support, and against defences now stronger and more strongly manned than the original first line. The attack broke down at or before this uncut obstacle, and the survivors turned and flowed backwards.
>
> Sir Basil Liddell-Hart, *A History of the World War*, 1930

AFTER THE BATTLE

By the end of the month we had seen more suffering and
death than it is good for men to see in a life time.
James Norman Hall, *Kitchener's Mob*, 1915

The first two days of the battle had been decisive. There would be
no spectacular breakthrough of the German lines. Instead, Loos
would continue in a desultory manner into October. Most of the
attacks would be limited, as would their aims, and they would
simply add to the mounting casualties.

By the close of action on 26 September the line had been
stabilised by the arrival of the experienced troops of the Guards
Division, as well as the 3rd Cavalry Division. North of the Guards,
however, in the vicinity of the hotly contested ground either side
of the Vermelles–Hulluch road, the men of the 9th Division, and
particularly the three battalions of the 24th Division (73rd Brigade:
9th Royal Sussex, 12th Royal Fusiliers and 7th Northants), were in a
parlous state. Exhausted, and without much food and water since
coming up into their advanced positions, their grip on the line
was tenuous. It would be severely tested in the early hours of the
27th, when the Germans counter-attacked at The Dump and the
Hohenzollern Redoubt. With The Dump lost, and *Fosse 8* behind

48. The ruins of Loos with 'Tower Bridge' in the distance.

it, the redoubt was severely threatened. Major General Thesiger, 9th Division, would be killed in an attempt to review the situation; his loss added to the growing roster of senior casualties during this battle. Fortunately, reinforced by men of the 5th Camerons and 8th Black Watch from the 9th Division (26th Brigade), the redoubt, already hard fought over, would be saved.

For his part, General Haig's plans for the 27th had centred on securing his fragile front, the steady hands of the Lord Cavan's Guards Division ensuring that this aim would be met. However, the glowering lump of Hill 70 and the shattered remains of the village of Hulluch still remained in German hands, reminders of the failed attempt to pierce fatally the enemy's lines. Cavan and XI Corps commander General Haking still regarded Hill 70 as a realistic target for a limited offensive to be resumed on 28 September. The objectives were shrinking, the opportunities for a major breakthrough lost. The all-out offensive originally planned was now distilling down to a classic bite-and-hold approach. Whether this hill could be bitten off and held by the British was another matter. After a limited bombardment, the Guards reached the hill, Bois Hugo still presenting a problem on the left flank of the operation. Nevertheless, the topography of the hill was to play its part, as described by the official historian:

> From the summit the lower part of Hill 70 is dead ground, the chalk slope being convex, and at first few casualties were incurred, but on reaching the upper part a violent machine-gun fire swept the lines. Casualties were at once extremely heavy, and after a few short rushes no further progress was possible. Every effort to move on again brought a burst of fire and further slaughter.
>
> Brigadier General Sir James Edmonds

With the Guards held in this difficult position, the 47th Division assaulted Chalk Pit Copse, to the west of the Lens–La Bassée road, in front of the hill. Preceded by an effective artillery bombardment, the Londoners were able to secure the wood. To the north, at Cuinchy, a gas attack was to clear the way for the 2nd Division to make some progress against the still intractable German lines. Once again, with a poverty of contours, the gas refused to budge eastwards; the 2nd Division wisely declined to leave their trenches. Another day had gone by, and the chances of any progress were limited. The battle had long since run out of steam.

The British commander-in-chief was now placed in a difficult position; with the resources having been expended on this costly gamble, Sir John French was forced to contact Joffre to ask for assistance. The French offensive in Artois had reached its high-water mark, at Point 140 on Vimy Ridge on 28 September, and the commander of the French Tenth Army, General d'Urbal, had

LT JOHN KIPLING

Rudyard Kipling's son, Lt John Kipling, of the 3rd Battalion, Irish Guards, was posted missing on 27 September, during the assault of the Guards Division. He was last seen close to Chalk Pit Wood. Though the famous author spent the rest of his life searching for his son, it was not until 1992 that a grave in St Marys ADS Cemetery was marked for John Kipling. Some historians dispute the accuracy of this identification.

49. *The grave of Lt John Kipling, St Mary's ADS Cemetery.*

hoped to press on with all his resources. The British converged with the French Army to the south of Loos, and here, as previously agreed, and with the town of Lens in the way, the French IX Corps stood on the defensive, its 152nd Division in reserve; it was the 152nd that was now the point of contention. With General d'Urbal eyeing this reserve division, it was General Foch, commander of the northern armies, who determined that the offensives should be held until there could be active co-ordination between the French and British forces. Foch had agreed to relieve the situation for Sir John by moving the French IX Corps up to take on the village of Loos, as well as the looming presence of Hill 70 behind. The French now took over the line at Loos; together the British XI Corps – now reinforced by two Territorial divisions, the 12th (Eastern) and 46th (North Midland), which replaced the shattered 21st and 24th divisions – and the French IX Corps would take on the assault against Hill 70 and the German second line. The attack would attempt to punch through the salient created by the German line in this position; but this ambition would be severely curtailed by the fact that the Germans still held on tightly to their positions at Hulluch, *Fosse 8* and The Dump. The British would have to attempt clearing these positions first; they would remain open sores that the Germans continued to pick away at with constant shelling and incessant attacks with hand grenades. In order to cap this, slowly, the Germans started to gain control of the approaches to the Hohenzollern Redoubt, the heavily entrenched position that had always been viewed as a major sticking point. The redoubt would fall, once again, into enemy hands, retaken by them on 3 October; only the southern trench extension, 'Big Willie', would remain in British hands. The barricaded join would be a difficult position to hold in the face of grenade attacks:

There were nightly bombing affairs, some of them the most desperate hand-to-hand contests for the possession of small

sectors of trench. The game of pitch and toss over the
barricades … continued for several days without a decision.

Pte James Norman Hall, 9th Royal Fusiliers

The gradual erosion of the Allied hold was to have a major impact
on the planning for a renewed Anglo-French offensive. Originally
slated for 2 October, it was to be put back, first to the 3rd and
then, in the light of the losses of the strongpoints in the northern
part of the line, to 6 October. Preparations were made. New start
trenches were dug and a new round of gas cylinders were laid.
Sir John moved the date of attack once more to 9 October; for
his part, General d'Urbal was to postpone the French attack to
the 10th, citing the need to relieve his III Corps. The offensive was
slipping out of the grasp of the Allied commanders; their hold on
what was left of their new positions, tenuous. For their part, the
Germans counter-attacked at Loos, but this assault was held by
the French. To the north, continued grenade attacks pressed the
British at the critical positions at The Dump and the quarries. The
Guards would hold on grimly. With Joffre hoping to resume his
offensives in Artois and the Champagne at the same time, the
delays were becoming a major issue. The slippage continued; the
battle would be resumed on 13 October.

The attack of 13 October would effectively mark the close
of the Battle of Loos (though the official halt would be called
on 6 November). It was a failure. There was a preliminary
bombardment on two days prior to the attack. Gas was again to
be released as a prelude to the attack, from over 3,000 cylinders;
with the wind conditions ideal it was nevertheless to have limited
effect as the gas dissipated. The German defence remained
stalwart in the face of attacks by the fresh British divisions that
had joined the XI Corps, to the north of the Vermelles–Hulluch
road: the 46th Division against the intractable Hohenzollern
Redoubt and The Dump; the 12th against the quarries. To the
south of the road, it was the 1st Division that would assault the

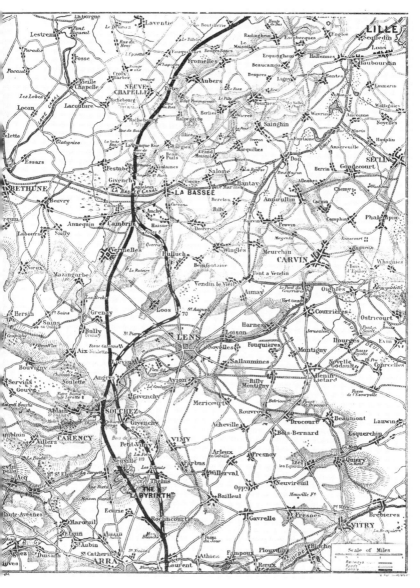

50. Map of the Anglo-French gains in Artois, 1915: Loos and Souchez.

German trenches parallel to the Lens–La Bassée road, north of Chalk Pit Copse, while in the southern sector the French would demonstrate against Hill 70 with their artillery. Zero hour was 2pm on a fine autumn day. The attack would fail:

> The Big Attack of Wednesday, the 13th, had been made, and contrary to the first messages that came through, had failed with very heavy losses. Only a part of the trench which formed the front of the Hohenzollern Redoubt was still held by our troops; the rest of the Redoubt was in German hands.
>
> Captain Roland Feilding, 3rd Coldstream Guards

The Battle of Loos was over.

THE LEGACY

Both Allies had gained in experience, if not wisdom, but they had afforded the Germans still better experience in the way to frustrate these attacks. And in 1916 it was the Germans who profited heavily both by the offensive and the defensive lesson.
Sir Basil Liddell-Hart, *A History of the World War*, 1930

The Battle of Loos saw the capture of this mining village – achieved on the first day – and the adjustment of the Allied line of just a few square miles. At the end of the three weeks of battle, the British had suffered 6,350 dead, including thirty-five senior officers and many more junior officers, and in total there would be some 50,380 casualties, over 2,000 of them officers. Casualties were high in the raw New Army battalions within the 15th Division – the Scots taking a particularly high number of losses – and in the 21st and 24th divisions that were pushed into the battle in such trying circumstances. While the Territorials of the 47th Division had achieved maximum penetration in the battle, the regulars of the 2nd Division were decimated – the last numbers of an already dying breed. The BEF would take some time to recover. The Germans would lose just under 20,000 men.

Joffre's grand plans were in tatters. With the British efforts intended to be taken in concert with the French advance south

51. Cheerful casualties. Served up for public consumption, this was the face of the British Army. The real losses would be staggering.

at Vimy Ridge, and farther south, with the great attack at the Champagne, hopes had been high – amongst the French at least. This would be a decisive breakthrough, a chance to win the war – or at least to put the Germans on the back foot, reeling back through the flat plain of Douai with the Allies in hot pursuit. However, the French Battle of Artois would run out of steam; though the French Tenth Army would take the village of Souchez, they would fail in their attempt of carrying the high

BLACKPOOL'S 'LOOS TRENCHES'

Show trenches dug in the seaside town of Blackpool were named 'Loos Trenches', becoming a tourist attraction. Wounded and convalescing soldiers from the battle were on hand as 'official guides' to show the public around.

52. The 'Loos Trenches', a tourist attraction at Blackpool. The reality would be less rosy.

53. The killing fields of the Champagne; German casualties examined by French officers.

ground of Vimy and Neuville St Vaast. As at Loos, the German second line was to hold firm. In the Champagne, the weight of the French artillery bombardment was to promise great results; the French advanced their line 2 miles in the first half-hour before running out of steam in the face of German reinforcement. German counter-attacks would later recapture the initial gains; the French lost 148,000 men in the two offensives. Joffre would later lose his position; the pressure was building on Sir John French, who would fall first.

Neither the British commander-in-chief, Sir John French, nor the general in charge of the attack, Sir Douglas Haig, wanted to fight at Loos. Despite Joffre's view to the contrary, the ground was poor, the strength of the German positions, holed up in fortified mining villages and slagheaps, just too great. With the Allied strategic situation in a parlous state, the Russians on the point of collapse, the need to support the French was recognised by the Secretary of State, Field Marshal Lord Kitchener. Stuck between Joffre and Kitchener, French and Haig had little choice but to attack where the British line met that of their Allies, just to the north of Lens.

54. British wounded awaiting evacuation after the battle.

In the aftermath of the first two days of battle, the contrary decision made by Sir John to retain control of XI Corps, and to hold it close to his chest and his headquarters, was to be a crucial one. It was almost as if Sir John, forced into this battle, remained reluctant to commit all of his resources to it. Sir Douglas, initially sceptical, was brought around in a wave of optimism with the chance of using poison gas for the first time against the Germans. To him, a limited operation had now become the opportunity to break the line using a new and terrible weapon of war: gas. With hopes that gas would magnify the limited effect of the British artillery, his plans included the very divisions held back by French.

For Kitchener's men, the Battle of Loos would have a varied impact. For the Scots of the 9th and 15th divisions, men of the 'First Hundred Thousand', it would mean action for the first time. In the language of the day, Ian Hay would describe the action of the 9th Division:

141

So ended our share in the Big Push. It was a small episode, spread over quite a short period, in one of the biggest and longest battles in the history of the world. The battle which began upon that grey September morning [raged] for nearly three weeks ... [surging] backwards and forwards over the same stricken mile of ground.

Ian Hay, *The First Hundred Thousand*, 1915

For the men of the 21st and 24th divisions it would spell disaster. On the move almost continuously since their arrival in France in early September, their movement into the battle front would be fraught with confusion, hold ups and congestion. Thrust into the line to resume the battle on 26 September, they would be tired, hungry and inexperienced, yet would be ordered to take on the most difficult part of the line. Forced between a bottle neck of two strongpoints of Hulluch and Hill 70, the novice divisions would be expected to assault the German second line, bristling with strongpoints, and enfiladed by advanced machine-gun fire. With little in the way of artillery preparation, sleep or rations, the assault would fail, the divisions broken. The corps commander, Major General Haking, would blame the poor march discipline of his troops, but the reality of their trials in battle would surely have challenged even the most experienced soldiers.

The controversy over the assignment and movement of the reserves would lead to a battle of a different sort: a clash between Sir Douglas Haig and Sir John French. Following the disaster on 28 September, Haig wrote to Kitchener to protest Sir John's intransigence in releasing the reserves to his command earlier. In Haig's view, but for the late arrival of the XI Corps divisions, the battle could have been won. However, given the strength of the German second-line defences and the weakness of the British artillery, this is unlikely. Haig's impatience is understandable, but his expectation that the battle could have been his for the taking is perhaps indicative of naïve optimism, even for the time. This battle

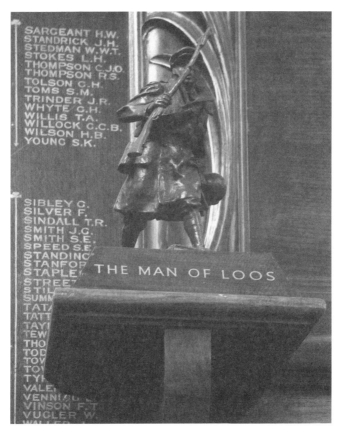

55. The Man of Loos; the London Irish war memorial.

would, however, sow the first seeds of the defeat of the German armies in 1918. Nevertheless, Haig had also sown the seeds of doubt in the abilities of Sir John French. The affair became played out in the press, with accusations and recriminations. Sir John would be out of his job; Haig's appointment as commander-in-chief BEF was announced on 10 December.

In one respect, the breaking of the German lines, Loos was a complete failure – but one that has helped focus the minds of military historians since the publication of Alan Clark's controversial book *The Donkeys*, published in 1961 and thought to be the primary influence for Joan Littlewood's production *Oh! What a Lovely War!* Both would help define a view of the Great War that lingers on today; that the generals were 'butchers and bunglers' and that their plans were hopelessly outdated and completely out of touch with the man on the ground. However, this biased view is out of step with the reality. When the British armies were to fight on their own terms, on ground of their own choosing, the victories would stack up. The learning curve, steep at first, would come good in 1918. Nevertheless, Loos was one of its most important steps on the way to the British Army's advance to victory in 1918.

ORDERS OF BATTLE

British Army

British Expeditionary Force (Commander-in-Chief, Field Marshal Sir John French)

First Army (General Sir Douglas Haig)

I Corps (Lieutenant General H. Gough)

2nd Division (Major General H. Horne)
5th Brigade (Brigadier General C.E. Corkran)
        1st Queen's
        2nd Oxfordshire & Buckinghamshire Light Infantry
        1/7th King's
        2nd Worcestershire
        2nd Highland Light Infantry (HLI)
6th Brigade (Brigadier General A.C. Daly)
        1st King's
        1st Royal Berkshire
        1/5th King's
        2nd South Staffordshire

1st KRRC
1/1st Herts
19th Brigade (Brigadier General P.R. Robertson)
2nd Royal Welsh Fusiliers
1st Middlesex
1/5th Scottish Rifles
1st Scottish Rifles
2nd Argyll & Sutherland Highlanders
4 RFA brigades (8 field-gun batteries, 2 howitzer batteries)
3 field companies RE
B Squadron, South Irish Horse
Cyclist company

7th Division (Major General T. Capper†)
20th Brigade (Brigadier General J.F. Hepburn-Stuart-Forbes-Trefusis)
2nd Border
8th Devonshire
1/6th Gordon Highlanders
2nd Gordon Highlanders
9th Devonshire
21st Brigade (Brigadier General H.E. Watts)
2nd Bedfordshire
2nd Royal Scots Fusiliers
1/4th Cameronians
2nd Yorkshire
2nd Wiltshire
22nd Brigade (Brigadier General J. McC. Steele)
2nd Queen's
1st Royal Welsh Fusiliers
2nd Royal Warwickshire
1st South Staffordshire
1 RHA brigade

3 RFA brigades (6 field-gun batteries, 2 howitzer batteries)
3 field companies RE
HQ and A Squadrons, Northumberland Hussars
Cyclist company

9th (Scottish) Division (Major General G. Thesiger†)
26th Brigade (Brigadier General A.B. Ritchie)
  8th Black Watch
  8th Gordon Highlanders
  7th Seaforth Highlanders
  5th Cameron Highlanders
27th Brigade (Brigadier General C.D. Bruce)
  11th Royal Scots
  6th Royal Scots Fusiliers
  12th Royal Scots
  10th Argyll & Sutherland Highlanders
28th Brigade (Brigadier General S.C. Scrase-Dickens)
  6th KOSB
  10th HLI
  9th Scottish Rifles
  11th HLI
4 RFA brigades (12 field-gun batteries, 3 howitzer batteries)
3 field companies RE
Pioneers: 9th Seaforths
B Squadron, Glasgow Yeomanry
Cyclist company
10 Motor Machine Gun (MMG) battery

28th Division (Major General E. Bulfin)
83rd Brigade (Brigadier General H.S.L. Ravenshaw)
  2nd King's Own
  1st KOYLI
  1/5th King's Own
  2nd East Yorkshire
  1/Welsh

147

IV Corps (Lieutenant General Sir H. Rawlinson)

1st Division (Major General A.E.A. Holland)
1st Brigade (Brigadier General A.J. Reddie)
   1st Black Watch
   10th Gloucestershire
   1/14th London (London Scottish)
   1st Camerons
   8th Royal Berkshire
2nd Brigade (Brigadier General J.H.W. Pollard)
   2nd Royal Sussex
   1st Loyal North Lancashires
   1/9th King's
   1st Northamptonshire
   2nd KRRC
3rd Brigade (Brigadier General H.R. Davies)
   1st South Wales Borderers
   2nd Welsh
   1st Gloucestershire
   2nd Royal Munster Fusiliers
4 RFA brigades (8 field-gun batteries, 2 howitzer batteries)
3 RE field companies
B Squadron, Northumberland Hussars
Cyclist company

15th (Scottish) Division (Major General F.W.N. MacCracken)
44th Brigade (Brigadier General M.G. Wilkinson)
   9th Black Watch
   10th Gordons
   8th Seaforths
   7th Camerons
45th Brigade (Brigadier General F.E. Wallerston)
   13th Royal Scots
   6th Camerons

7th Royal Scots Fusiliers

11th Argyll & Sutherland Highlanders

46th Brigade (Brigadier General T.G. Matheson)

7th KOSB

10th Scottish Rifles

8th KOSB

12th HLI

4 RFA brigades (12 field-gun batteries, 4 howitzer batteries)

3 RE field companies

Pioneers: 9th Gordons

B Squadron, Westmorland & Cumberland Yeomanry

Cyclist company

47th (London) Division (Major General C. St L. Barter)

140th Brigade (Brigadier General G.J. Cuthbert)

1/6th London (City of London)

1/8th London (Post Office Rifles)

1/7th London (City of London)

1/15th London (Civil Service Rifles)

141st Brigade (Brigadier General W. Thwaites)

1/17th London (Poplar & Stepney Rifles)

1/19th London (St Pancras)

1/18th London (London Irish)

1/20th London (Blackheath & Woolwich)

142nd Brigade (Brigadier General F.G. Lewis)

1/21th London (1st Surrey Rifles)

1/23th London

1/22th London (The Queen's)

1/24th London (The Queen's)

4 RFA brigades (9 field-gun batteries, 2 howitzer batteries)

3 RE field companies

Pioneers: 1/4th Royal Welsh Fusiliers

C Squadron, King Edward's Horse

Cyclist company

XI Corps (Lieutenant General R.C.B. Haking)

Guards Division (Major General F.R. Earl of Cavan)
1st Guards Brigade (Brigadier General G.P.T. Feilding)
       2nd Grenadier Guards
       3rd Coldstream Guards
       2nd Coldstream Guards
       1st Irish Guards
2nd Guards Brigade (Brigadier General J. Ponsonby)
       3rd Grenadier Guards
       1st Scots Guards
       1st Coldstream Guards
       2nd Irish Guards
3rd Guards Brigade (Brigadier General F.J. Heyworth)
       1st Grenadier Guards
       2nd Scots Guards
       4th Grenadier Guards
       1st Welsh Guards
4 RFA brigades (12 field-gun batteries, 4 howitzer batteries)
3 RE field companies
Pioneers: 4th Coldstream Guards
Household Cavalry Squadron
Cyclist company

12th (Eastern) Division (Major General F.D.V. Wing†) (replaced 21st Division, 29 September)
35th Brigade (Brigadier General C.H.C. van Straubenzee)
       7th Norfolk
       9th Essex
       7th Suffolk
       5th Royal Berkshire
36th Brigade (Brigadier General H.B. Borradaile)
       8th Royal Fusiliers
       7th Royal Sussex

9th Royal Fusiliers

11th Middlesex

37th Brigade (Brigadier General C.A. Fowler)

6th Queen's

7th East Surrey

6th Buffs

6th Royal West Kent

4 RFA brigades (12 field-gun batteries, 3 howitzer batteries)

3 RE field companies

Pioneers: 5th Northamptonshire

HQ Machine Gun Section

A Squadron, King Edward's Horse

Cyclist company

9th MMG Battery

21st Division (Major General G.T. Forestier–Walker)

62nd Brigade (Brigadier General E.B. Wilkinson)

12th Northumberland Fusiliers

8th East Yorkshire

13th Northumberland Fusiliers

10th Yorkshire

63rd Brigade (Brigadier General N.T. Nickalls†)

8th Lincolnshire

12th West Yorkshire

8th Somerset Light Infantry

10th York & Lancashire

64th Brigade (Brigadier General G.M. Gloster)

9th KOYLI

14th DLI

10th KOYLI

15th DLI

4 RFA brigades (12 field-gun batteries, 4 howitzer batteries)

3 RE field companies

Pioneers: 14th Northumberland Fusiliers

A Squadron, South Irish Horse
Cyclist company

24th Division (Major General Sir J.G. Ramsay)
71st Brigade (Brigadier General M.T. Shewen)
        9th Norfolk
        8th Bedfordshire
        9th Suffolk
        11th Essex
72nd Brigade (Brigadier General B.R. Mitford)
        8th Queen's
        9th East Surrey
        8th Buffs
        8th Royal West Kent
73rd Brigade (Brigadier General W.A. Oswald)
        12th Royal Fusiliers
        7th Northamptonshire
        9th Royal Sussex
        13th Middlesex
4 RFA brigades (12 field-gun batteries, 4 howitzer batteries)
3 RE field companies
Pioneers: 12th Sherwood Foresters
A Squadron, Glasgow Yeomanry
Cyclist company

46th (North Midland) Division (Major General Hon. E.J. Montagu-Stuart-Wortley) (replaced 24th Division, 3 October)
137th Brigade (Brigadier General E. Feetham)
   1/5th South Staffordshire
   1/5th North Staffordshire
   1/6th South Staffordshire
   1/6th North Staffordshire
138th Brigade (Brigadier General G.C. Kemp)
   1/4th Lincolnshire

1/4th Leicestershire
1/5th Lincolnshire
1/5th Leicestershire
139th Brigade (Brigadier General C.T. Shipley)
1/5th Sherwood Foresters
1/7th Sherwood Foresters
1/6th Sherwood Foresters
1/8th Sherwood Foresters
4 RFA brigades (9 field-gun batteries, 2 howitzer batteries)
3 RE field companies
Pioneers: 1/1st Monmouthshire
B Squadron, Yorkshire Hussars
Cyclist company

† Killed in action or mortally wounded during the battle

German Army

Sixth Army (Crown Prince Rupprecht)

IV. Armeekorps (General Sixt von Armin)

Korps artillery
6 howitzer (5.9in) batteries
1.5 mortar (11in) batteries
3 field-gun batteries (4in, 4.8in, 5.9in)

117th Division

157th (8th Lorraine) Regiment
22nd Reserve Regiment
11th Reserve Regiment
6 field artillery batteries
3 light howitzer artillery batteries

14th Division

16th (3rd Westphalian) Regiment
56th (7th Westphalian) Regiment
57th (8th Westphalian) Regiment
11th (Hessian) *Jäger* Battalion
9 field artillery batteries
3 light howitzer artillery batteries

FURTHER READING

Unlike some battles of the Great War, Loos has had indifferent coverage. Most recommended of the books below are the *Official History* of the late 1920s and the intelligent analysis by Nick Lloyd, as well as a few of the contemporary accounts that provide the accurate voices of the combatants. The most controversial account, however, remains that of Alan Clark. Still in print, this book that has done much to foster the image, now largely discredited, of the British Army in 1915 as 'lions led by donkeys'.

Cherry, Niall, *Most Unfavourable Ground. The Battle of Loos 1915* (Helion, 2005)

Clark, Alan, *The Donkeys* (Pimlico, 1993)

Corrigan, Gordon, *Loos 1915, The Unwanted Battle* (Spellmount, 2005)

Dunn, J.C., *The War the Infantry Knew, 1914–1919* (Abacus, 2004)

Edmonds, Brigadier General Sir James, *Military Operations, France & Belgium, 1915, Volume 1* (Macmillan, 1927)

———, *Military Operations, France & Belgium, 1915, Volume 2* (Macmillan, 1928)

Feilding, Rowland, *War Letters to a Wife* (Medici Society, 1929)

Foulkes, Major General C.H., *'Gas!' The Story of the Special Brigade* (William Blackwood, 1934)

Graves, Robert, *Goodbye to All That* (Penguin, 1960)

Griffth, Paddy (ed.), *British Fighting Methods in the Great War* (Frank Cass, 1996)

Hall, James Norman, *Kitchener's Mob* (Houghton Mifflin, 1916)

Harris, Ed, *The Footballer of Loos* (The History Press, 2009)

Hay, Ian, *The First Hundred Thousand* (William Blackwood, 1915)

Lloyd, Nick, *Loos 1915* (The History Press, 2006)

MacGill, Patrick, *The Great Push* (Herbert Jenkins, 1915)

Richter, R., *Chemical Soldiers: British Gas Warfare in World War 1* (University of Kansas Press, 1992)

Warner, Phillip, *The Battle of Loos* (William Kimber, 1976)

INDEX

EXPLORE HISTORY'S MAJOR CONFLICTS WITH
BATTLE STORY